plurall

Parabéns!
Agora você faz parte do **Plurall**, a plataforma digital do seu livro didático! Acesse e conheça todos os recursos e funcionalidades disponíveis para as suas aulas digitais.

Baixe o aplicativo do **Plurall** para Android e IOS ou acesse **www.plurall.net** e cadastre-se utilizando o seu código de acesso exclusivo:

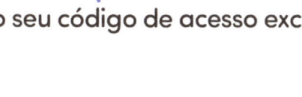

AAABY58DS

Este é o seu código de acesso Plurall. Cadastre-se e ative-o para ter acesso aos conteúdos relacionados a esta obra.

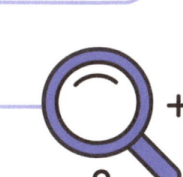

@plurallnet

@plurallnetoficial

ENSINO FUNDAMENTAL • ANOS INICIAIS

Eliete Canesi Morino

Graduada em Língua e Literatura Inglesa e Tradução e Interpretação pela Pontifícia Universidade Católica de São Paulo (PUC-SP).

Especialização em Língua Inglesa pela International Bell School of London.

Pós-graduada em Metodologia da Língua Inglesa pela Faculdade de Tecnologia e Ciência (FTC-SP).

Atuou como professora da rede particular de ensino e em projetos comunitários.

Rita Brugin de Faria

Graduada pela Faculdade de Arte Santa Marcelina e pela Faculdade Paulista de Arte, ambas em São Paulo (SP).

Especialização em Língua Inglesa pela International Bell School of London.

Pós-graduada em Metodologia da Língua Inglesa pela Faculdade de Tecnologia e Ciência (FTC-SP).

Especialista em alfabetização, atuou como professora e coordenadora pedagógica das redes pública e particular de ensino.

Áudios

Escaneie o *QR Code* para ter acesso aos áudios deste volume e do *reader* que o acompanha.

Presidência: Mario Ghio Júnior

Vice-presidência de educação digital: Camila Montero Vaz Cardoso

Direção editorial: Lidiane Vivaldini Olo

Gerência editorial: Julio Cesar Augustus de Paula Santos

Coordenação editorial: Luciana Nicoleti

Edição: Ana Lucia Militello

Aprendizagem digital: Renata Galdino (ger.), Beatriz de Almeida Pinto Rodrigues da Costa (coord. de Experiência de aprendizagem), Carla Isabel Ferreira Reis (coord. de Produção multimídia), Daniela dos Santos Di Nubila (coord. de Produção digital), Rogério Fabio Alves (coord. de Publicação) e Vanessa Tavares Menezes de Souza (coord. de Design digital)

Planejamento, controle de produção e indicadores: Flávio Matuguma (ger.), Juliana Batista (coord.) e Jayne Ruas (analista)

Revisão: Letícia Pieroni (coord.), Aline Cristina Vieira, Anna Clara Razvickas, Carla Bertinato, Daniela Lima, Danielle Modesto, Diego Carbone, Elane Vicerite, Kátia S. Lopes Godoi, Lilian M. Kumai, Malvina Tomáz, Marília H. Lima, Patrícia Rocco S. Renda, Paula Freire, Paula Rubia Baltazar, Paula Teixeira, Raquel A. Taveira, Ricardo Miyake, Shirley Figueiredo Ayres, Tayra Alfonso e Thaise Rodrigues

Arte: Fernanda Costa da Silva (ger.), Catherine Saori Ishihara (coord.) e Kuiasu Vuzu Whikalil (edição de arte)

Diagramação: Ile Comunicação Eireli

Iconografia e tratamento de imagem: Roberta Bento (ger.), Claudia Bertolazzi (coord.), Roberta Freire Lacerda dos Santos (pesquisa iconográfica), Iron Mantovanello Oliveira e Fernanda Crevin (tratamento de imagens)

Licenciamento de conteúdo de terceiros: Roberta Bento (ger.), Jenis Oh (coord.) e Liliane Rodrigues (analista de licenciamento)

Ilustrações: Clau Souza, Estudio Ornitorrinco, Ilustra Cartoon, Marcos Mello, Sirayama e Superludico.

Cartografia: Eric Fuzii (coord.) e Robson da Rocha (edição de arte)

Design: Erik Taketa (coord.) e Talita Guedes da Silva (capa e proj. gráfico)

Ilustração da capa e logotipo: Superludico

Todos os direitos reservados por Somos Sistemas de Ensino S.A.
Avenida Paulista, 901, 6º andar – Bela Vista
São Paulo – SP – CEP 01310-200
http://www.somoseducacao.com.br

Dados Internacionais de Catalogação na Publicação (CIP)	**Dados Internacionais de Catalogação na Publicação (CIP)**

```
Faria, Rita Brugin de
  Hello! Kids 2° ano / Rita Brugin de Faria, Eliete Canesi
Morino. -- 6. ed. -- São Paulo : Ática, 2023.

  Suplementado pelo manual do professor.
  Bibliografia
  ISBN 978-85-0819-856-6 (aluno)
  ISBN 978-85-0819-852-8 (professor)

  1. Língua inglesa (Ensino fundamental) I. Morino, Eliete
Canesi II. Título

                                            CDD 372.652
22-0174
```

```
Faria, Rita Brugin de
  Hello! Kids 2° ano [livro eletrônico] / Rita Brugin de
Faria, Eliete Canesi Morino. -- 1. ed. -- São Paulo :
Ática, 2023.
  PDF

  Suplementado pelo manual do professor.
  Bibliografia
  ISBN 978-85-0819-846-7 (e-book) (aluno)
  ISBN 978-85-0819-841-2 (e-book) (professor)

  1. Língua inglesa (Ensino fundamental) I. Morino, Eliete
Canesi II. Título

22-0179                                    CDD 372.652
```

Angélica Ilacqua – Bibliotecária – CRB-8/7057

2025
Código CAE 792310 / OP 247943
6ª edição
4ª impressão
De acordo com a BNCC.

Impressão e acabamento: D'ARTHY Editora e Gráfica Ltda

CONTENTS

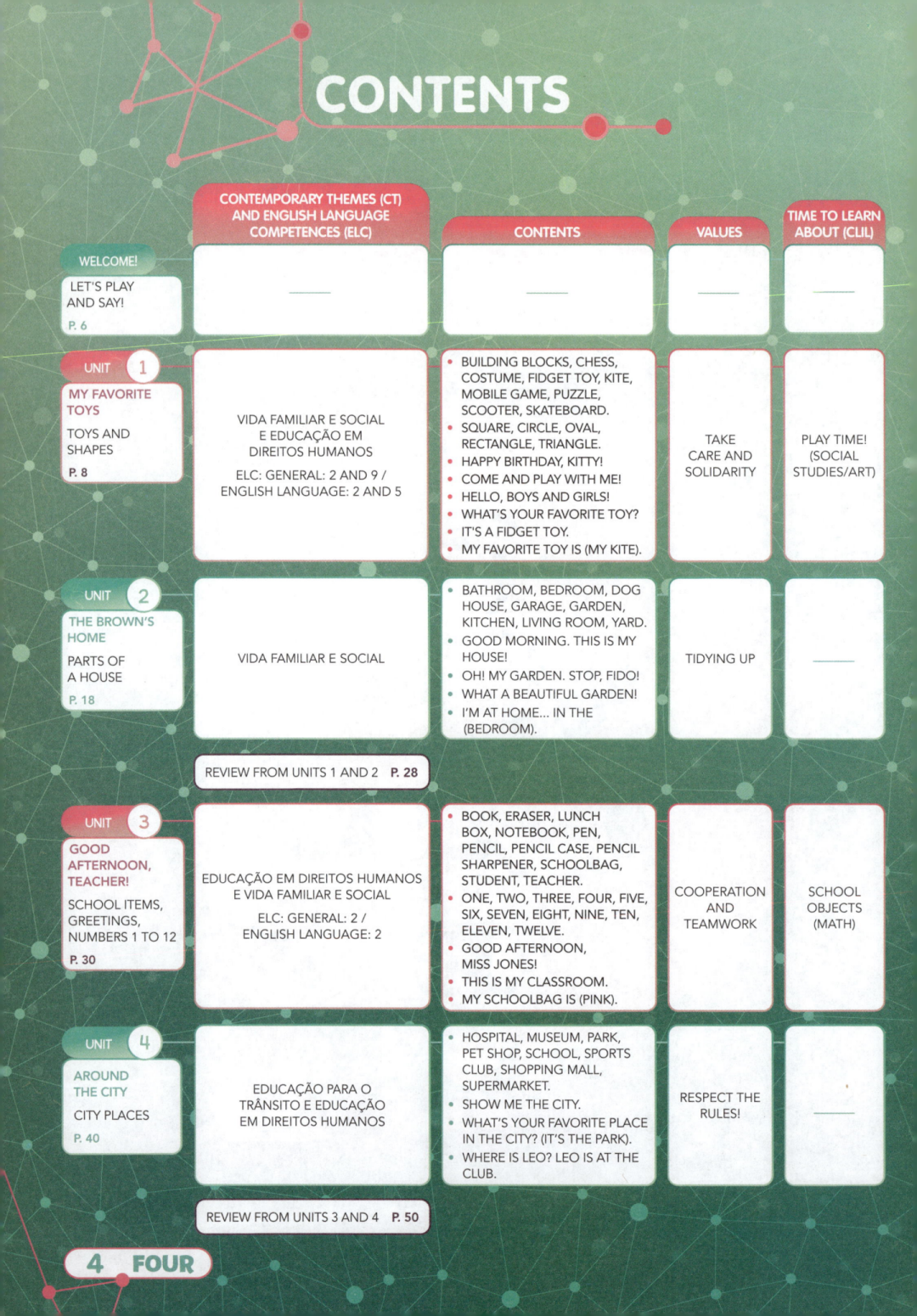

	CONTEMPORARY THEMES (CT) AND ENGLISH LANGUAGE COMPETENCES (ELC)	CONTENTS	VALUES	TIME TO LEARN ABOUT (CLIL)
WELCOME! LET'S PLAY AND SAY! **P. 6**	—	—	—	—
UNIT 1 **MY FAVORITE TOYS** TOYS AND SHAPES **P. 8**	VIDA FAMILIAR E SOCIAL E EDUCAÇÃO EM DIREITOS HUMANOS ELC: GENERAL: 2 AND 9 / ENGLISH LANGUAGE: 2 AND 5	• BUILDING BLOCKS, CHESS, COSTUME, FIDGET TOY, KITE, MOBILE GAME, PUZZLE, SCOOTER, SKATEBOARD. • SQUARE, CIRCLE, OVAL, RECTANGLE, TRIANGLE. • HAPPY BIRTHDAY, KITTY! • COME AND PLAY WITH ME! • HELLO, BOYS AND GIRLS! • WHAT'S YOUR FAVORITE TOY? • IT'S A FIDGET TOY. • MY FAVORITE TOY IS (MY KITE).	TAKE CARE AND SOLIDARITY	PLAY TIME! (SOCIAL STUDIES/ART)
UNIT 2 **THE BROWN'S HOME** PARTS OF A HOUSE **P. 18**	VIDA FAMILIAR E SOCIAL	• BATHROOM, BEDROOM, DOG HOUSE, GARAGE, GARDEN, KITCHEN, LIVING ROOM, YARD. • GOOD MORNING. THIS IS MY HOUSE! • OH! MY GARDEN. STOP, FIDO! • WHAT A BEAUTIFUL GARDEN! • I'M AT HOME... IN THE (BEDROOM).	TIDYING UP	
REVIEW FROM UNITS 1 AND 2 **P. 28**				
UNIT 3 **GOOD AFTERNOON, TEACHER!** SCHOOL ITEMS, GREETINGS, NUMBERS 1 TO 12 **P. 30**	EDUCAÇÃO EM DIREITOS HUMANOS E VIDA FAMILIAR E SOCIAL ELC: GENERAL: 2 / ENGLISH LANGUAGE: 2	• BOOK, ERASER, LUNCH BOX, NOTEBOOK, PEN, PENCIL, PENCIL CASE, PENCIL SHARPENER, SCHOOLBAG, STUDENT, TEACHER. • ONE, TWO, THREE, FOUR, FIVE, SIX, SEVEN, EIGHT, NINE, TEN, ELEVEN, TWELVE. • GOOD AFTERNOON, MISS JONES! • THIS IS MY CLASSROOM. • MY SCHOOLBAG IS (PINK).	COOPERATION AND TEAMWORK	SCHOOL OBJECTS (MATH)
UNIT 4 **AROUND THE CITY** CITY PLACES **P. 40**	EDUCAÇÃO PARA O TRÂNSITO E EDUCAÇÃO EM DIREITOS HUMANOS	• HOSPITAL, MUSEUM, PARK, PET SHOP, SCHOOL, SPORTS CLUB, SHOPPING MALL, SUPERMARKET. • SHOW ME THE CITY. • WHAT'S YOUR FAVORITE PLACE IN THE CITY? (IT'S THE PARK). • WHERE IS LEO? LEO IS AT THE CLUB.	RESPECT THE RULES!	—
REVIEW FROM UNITS 3 AND 4 **P. 50**				

CONTEMPORARY THEMES (CT) AND ENGLISH LANGUAGE COMPETENCES (ELC)

	CONTEMPORARY THEMES (CT) AND ENGLISH LANGUAGE COMPETENCES (ELC)	CONTENTS	VALUES	TIME TO LEARN ABOUT (CLIL)
UNIT 5				
AT THE BEACH	VIDA FAMILIAR E SOCIAL, EDUCAÇÃO AMBIENTAL E EDUCAÇÃO PARA O CONSUMO	• CLOUD, DOLPHIN, FISH, MOON, SANDCASTLE, SEA, SHARK, SEASHELL, SKY, STAR, STARFISH, SUN; IN THE MORNING, IN THE EVENING.	KEEP THE BEACHES CLEAN	BEACH SPORTS (PHYSICAL EDUCATION/ MATH)
BEACH AND NATURE ELEMENTS, PERIODS OF THE DAY, NUMBERS 10 TO 15	ELC: GENERAL: 4 / SPECIFIC: 3 / ENGLISH LANGUAGE: 2	• TEN, ELEVEN, TWELVE, THIRTEEN, FOURTEEN, FIFTEEN.		
P. 52		• GOOD MORNING! IT'S A BEAUTIFUL DAY!		
		• GOOD EVENING! IT'S A BEAUTIFUL NIGHT!		
UNIT 6		• ANT, BEE, FISH, FROG, PARROT, RABBIT, SNAIL, SNAKE, SQUIRREL, TURTLE.		
I LOVE ANIMALS!	EDUCAÇÃO AMBIENTAL E VIDA FAMILIAR E SOCIAL	• WHAT'S THAT? IS IT A (SNAKE)? YES, IT IS. / NO, IT ISN'T.	PROTECT THE PARROTS	
ANIMALS		• I LOVE ANIMALS!		
P. 62		• WHAT IS THIS? IT'S A (FISH)!		
		• WHAT ANIMAL IS IT?		

REVIEW FROM UNITS 5 AND 6 **P. 72**

UNIT 7	VIDA FAMILIAR E SOCIAL, EDUCAÇÃO ALIMENTAR E NUTRICIONAL E SAÚDE.	• APPLE, BANANA, BREAD, BUTTER, CAKE, COFFEE, EGG, MILK, ORANGE JUICE, SUGAR; NUMBERS: TEN, ELEVEN, TWELVE, THIRTEEN, FOURTEEN, FIFTEEN, SIXTEEN, SEVENTEEN, EIGHTEEN, NINETEEN, TWENTY.	EAT HEALTHY FOOD! NO WASTING!	THE FOOD WE EAT (SCIENCE)
TIME FOR BREAKFAST	ELC: GENERAL: 2 / SPECIFIC: 2 / ENGLISH LANGUAGE: 2	• ARE YOU HUNGRY, ALLAN?		
FOOD AND DRINKS, NUMBERS 10 TO 20		• OH, YES, I'M HUNGRY, DAD!		
P. 74		• EAT YOUR BREAKFAST, DEAR!		
UNIT 8		• ARM, EAR, EYE, FINGER, FOOT, HAIR, HAND, HEAD, LEG, MOUTH, NOSE, TOE.		
OUR BODY	SAÚDE	• WHAT COLOR IS YOUR HAIR? MY HAIR IS (RED).	TAKE CARE OF YOUR BODY	
THE HUMAN BODY		• WHAT COLOR ARE YOUR EYES? MY EYES ARE (BROWN).		
P. 84				

REVIEW FROM UNITS 7 AND 8 **P. 94**

EXTRA PRACTICE P. 96	WORKBOOK P. 113	HAPPY MOTHER'S DAY! P. 131	MERRY CHRISTMAS AND HAPPY NEW YEAR! P. 135
PROJECTS P. 104	CELEBRATION CRAFTS P. 129	HAPPY FATHER'S DAY! P. 133	MINI CARDS P. 137
GLOSSARY P. 108	HAPPY EASTER! P. 129	HAPPY THANKSGIVING DAY! P. 133	STICKERS P. 145
STRUCTURES P. 112	HAPPY FRIENDSHIP DAY! P. 131		

ICONS

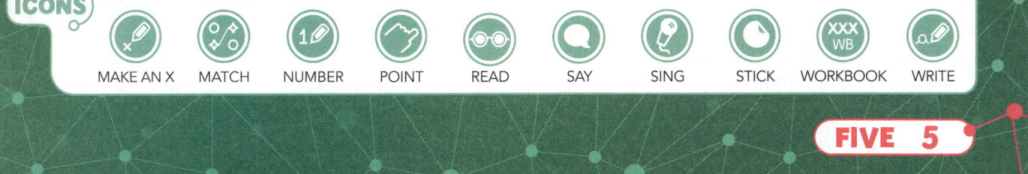

ACT OUT · CHECK · CIRCLE · COLOR · COUNT · CUT · DRAW · GLUE · LET'S TALK · LISTEN · MAKE AN X · MATCH · NUMBER · POINT · READ · SAY · SING · STICK · WORKBOOK · WRITE

UNIT 1 MY FAVORITE TOYS

1. LISTEN, POINT AND SAY.

2. LISTEN, STICK AND SAY.

3. LISTEN, POINT AND SAY.

WHAT'S YOUR FAVORITE TOY?

4. MATCH AND COLOR.

| SQUARE | CIRCLE | OVAL | RECTANGLE | TRIANGLE |

A A YELLOW RECTANGLE ●

B A GREEN TRIANGLE ●

C A BLUE CIRCLE ●

D A PINK OVAL ●

E A RED SQUARE ●

5. INTERVIEW YOUR FRIENDS. WHAT'S YOUR FAVORITE TOY?

		FRIEND'S NAME		
		FRIEND 1	**FRIEND 2**	**FRIEND 3**
		_____	_____	_____
	BUILDING BLOCKS			
	SCOOTER			
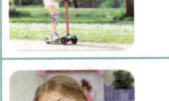	FIDGET TOY			
	COSTUME			
	CHESS			
	PUZZLE			
	MOBILE GAME			

Say with Me!

RECTANGLE, TRIANGLE, SQUARE, RECTANGLE, TRIANGLE, SQUARE. CARE, LET'S SHARE!

HAPPY BIRTHDAY!

HAPPY BIRTHDAY TO YOU,
HAPPY BIRTHDAY TO YOU,
HAPPY BIRTHDAY, DEAR KITTY,
HAPPY BIRTHDAY TO YOU! (2x)

6. LOOK AND NUMBER.

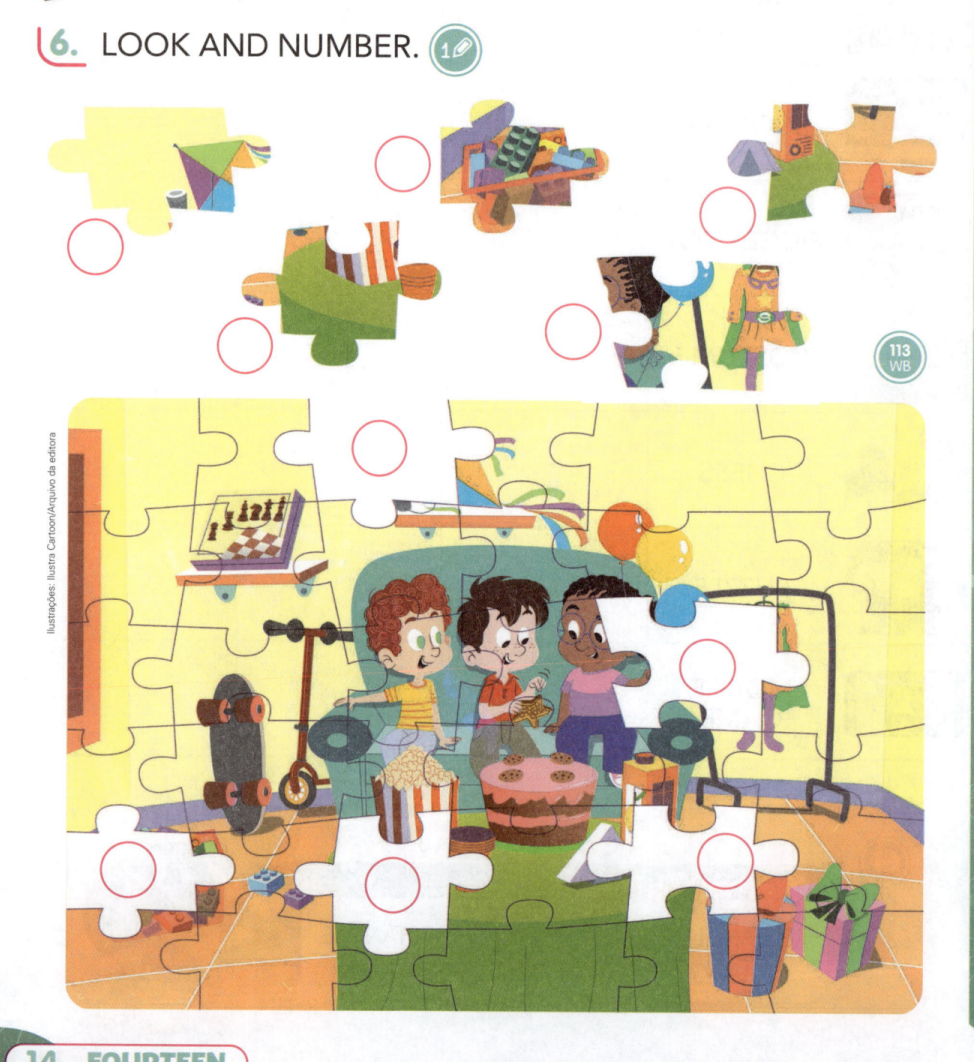

GROWING UP

TAKE CARE AND SOLIDARITY!

7. LOOK AT THE PICTURE AND TALK TO YOUR CLASSMATES. 👥

8. DRAW YOUR FAVORITE TOY AND ONE YOU CAN DONATE. ✏️

TIME TO LEARN ABOUT PLAY TIME!

WHAT IS YOUR FAVORITE TYPE OF PLAY?

1. LOOK AT THE PICTURES AND CIRCLE.

2. INTERVIEW A FAMILY MEMBER. THEN DRAW HIS OR HER FAVORITE TOY.

NOW, LET'S CREATE A SPECIAL TOY!

3. CREATE A TIC-TAC-TOE BOARD. THEN PLAY WITH YOUR CLASSMATES.

2. LISTEN, STICK AND SAY.

3. LISTEN, NUMBER AND SAY.

4. LOOK AND MAKE AN X.

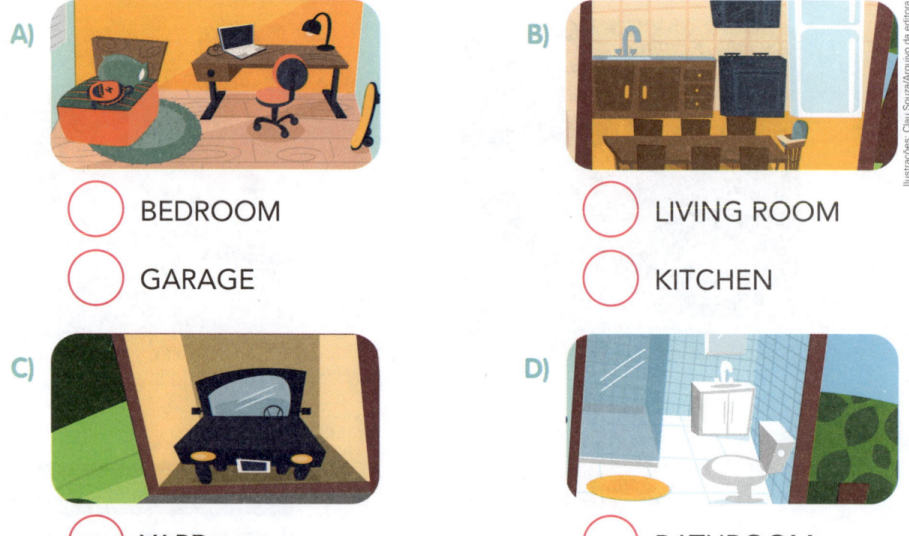

A)

- ◯ BEDROOM
- ◯ GARAGE

B)

- ◯ LIVING ROOM
- ◯ KITCHEN

C)

- ◯ YARD
- ◯ GARAGE

D)

- ◯ BATHROOM
- ◯ GARAGE

5. DRAW OR GLUE.

6. COLOR AND SAY.

7. READ AND COLOR. WHAT COLOR ARE THE BALLOONS?

8. OBSERVE THE PICTURES AND MATCH.

 ●   ●

 ●   ●

 ●   ●

 ●   ●

LET'S SING!

SWEET HOME

I'M AT HOME...
IN THE LIVING ROOM.
I'M AT HOME...
IN THE KITCHEN.
I'M AT HOME...
IN THE BATHROOM.
I'M AT HOME...
IN THE BEDROOM.
I'M AT HOME...
SWEET HOME! (2x)

9. SING. THEN LISTEN, CIRCLE AND SAY.

Say with Me!
A GARDEN, A KITCHEN... A PIGEON IN THE KITCHEN! YES! A PIGEON IN THE KITCHEN.

GROWING UP

TIDYING UP

10. LOOK AT THE PICTURE AND TALK TO YOUR CLASSMATES.

11. ROLE PLAY WITH YOUR FRIENDS A CLEAN-UP SITUATION AT HOME. DRAW.

CHECK YOUR PROGRESS

REVIEW

1. MATCH.

● ● CHESS

● ● KITE

● ● SCOOTER

● ● MOBILE GAME

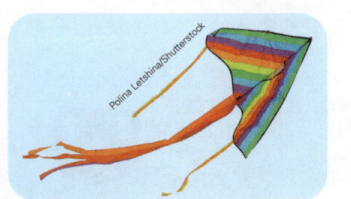

● ● SKATEBOARD

2. READ AND CIRCLE.

A) IT'S A KITCHEN / IT'S A BEDROOM.

B) IT'S A LIVING ROOM / IT'S A BEDROOM.

C) IT'S A BATHROOM / IT'S A GARAGE.

D) IT'S A LIVING ROOM / IT'S A KITCHEN.

E) IT'S A BEDROOM / IT'S A GARAGE.

F) IT'S A YARD / IT'S A BATHROOM.

2. LISTEN, STICK AND SAY.

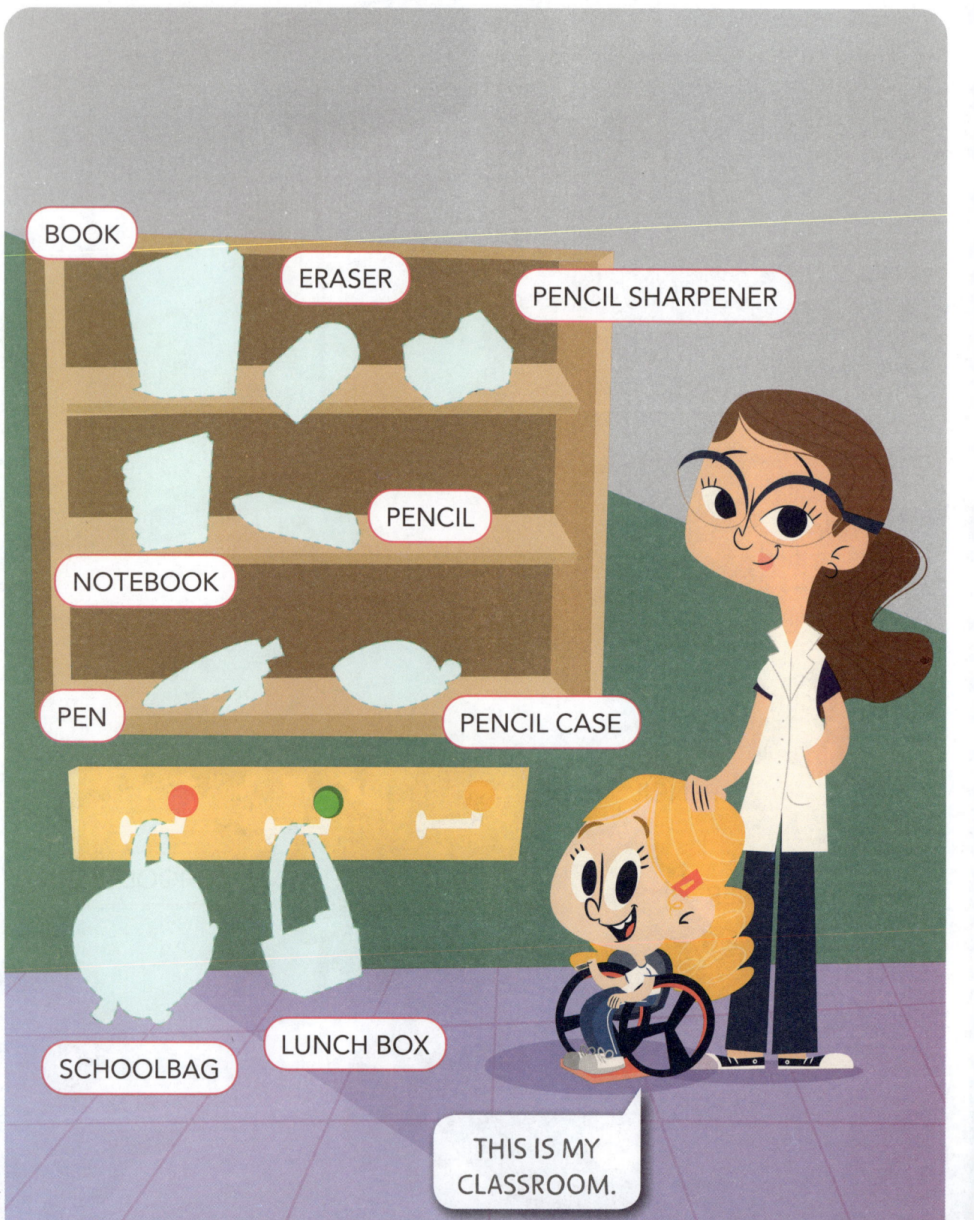

3. LISTEN AND COUNT.

4. LISTEN AND MAKE AN X.

5. READ AND WRITE.

THE NAME OF YOUR SCHOOL: _____

THE NAME OF YOUR ENGLISH TEACHER: _____

6. READ AND DRAW.

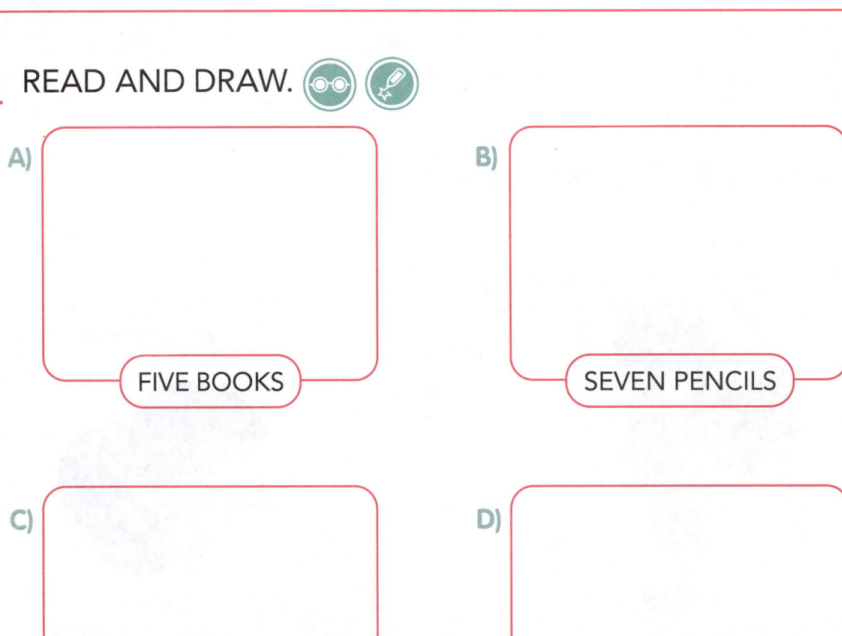

7. READ AND MAKE AN X.

A)

THIS IS A PENCIL SHARPENER.

YES ( )

NO ( )

B)

THIS IS A PEN.

YES ( )

NO ( )

C)

THIS IS A LUNCH BOX.

YES ( )

NO ( )

D)

THIS IS A PEN.

YES ( )

NO ( )

E)

THIS IS A BOOK.

YES ( )

NO ( )

F)

THIS IS A PENCIL CASE.

YES ( )

NO ( )

G)

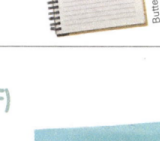

THIS IS A NOTEBOOK.

YES ( )

NO ( )

LET'S SING!

SCHOOL CHANT

PAPER, PENCIL,
ERASER, PEN.
I CAN WRITE
AND READ AGAIN. (4x)

8. CROSSWORD.

Say with Me!

I'M AT SCHOOL TO LEARN AND PLAY.
WHAT A HAPPY DAY!

GROWING UP

COOPERATION AND TEAMWORK

9. LOOK AT THE PICTURE AND TALK TO YOUR CLASSMATES.

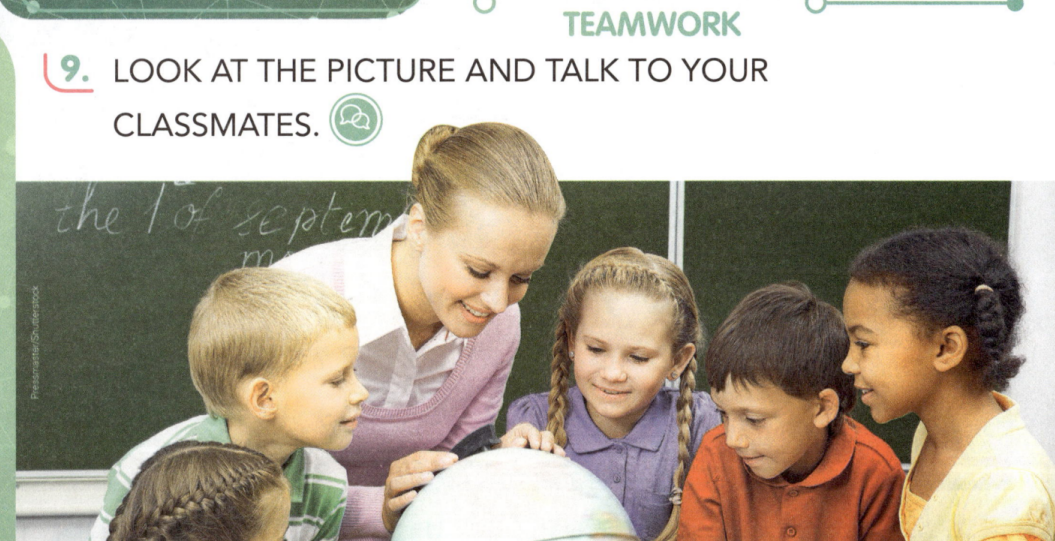

10. LET'S TALK ABOUT COOPERATION AND GOOD COEXISTENCE RULES WHEN WORKING IN GROUPS. CHOOSE THE BEST OF FIVE BELOW AND ILLUSTRATE THEM.

DO YOUR BEST • RESPECT DIFFERENT OPINIONS • BE A GOOD LISTENER • BE KIND • BE POSITIVE

TIME TO LEARN ABOUT

SCHOOL OBJECTS

WHAT ARE YOUR SCHOOL OBJECTS?

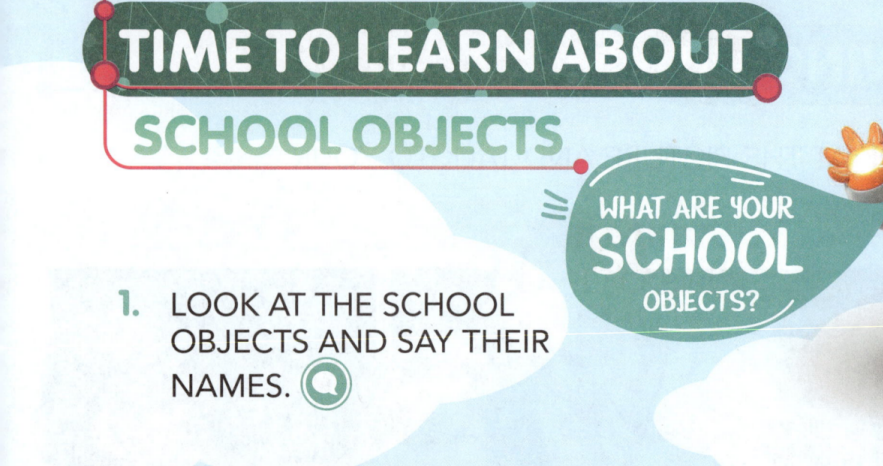

1. LOOK AT THE SCHOOL OBJECTS AND SAY THEIR NAMES.

2. LOOK, SAY AND COMPLETE.

MY NEW SCHOOL OBJECTS ARE...

3. DRAW, COUNT AND SAY.

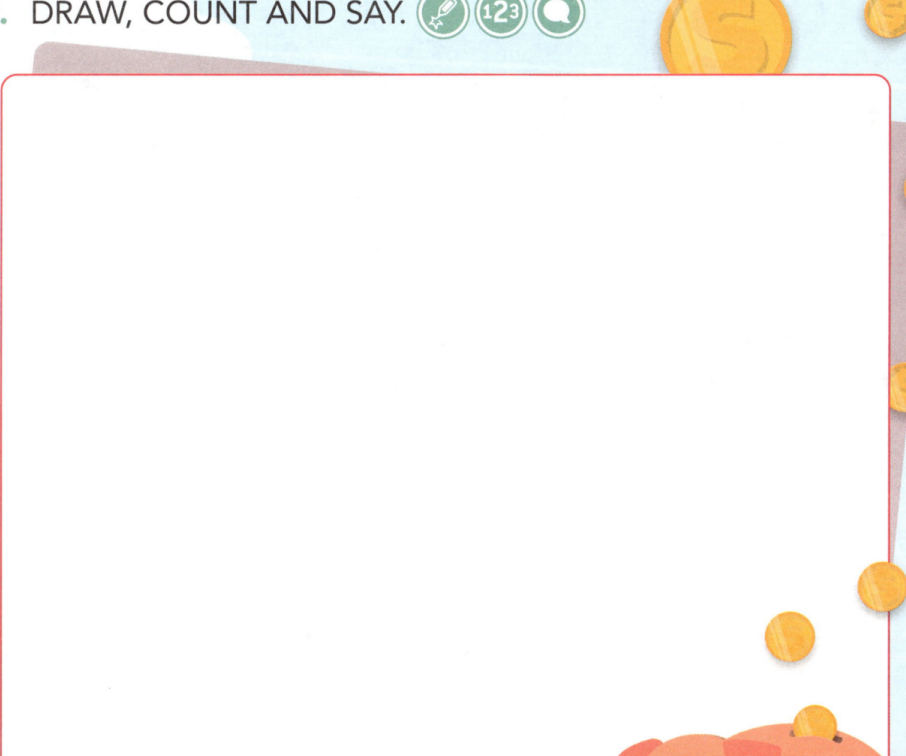

TOTAL: _____ KIDSTAKS

I HAVE LEFT _____ KIDSTAKS.

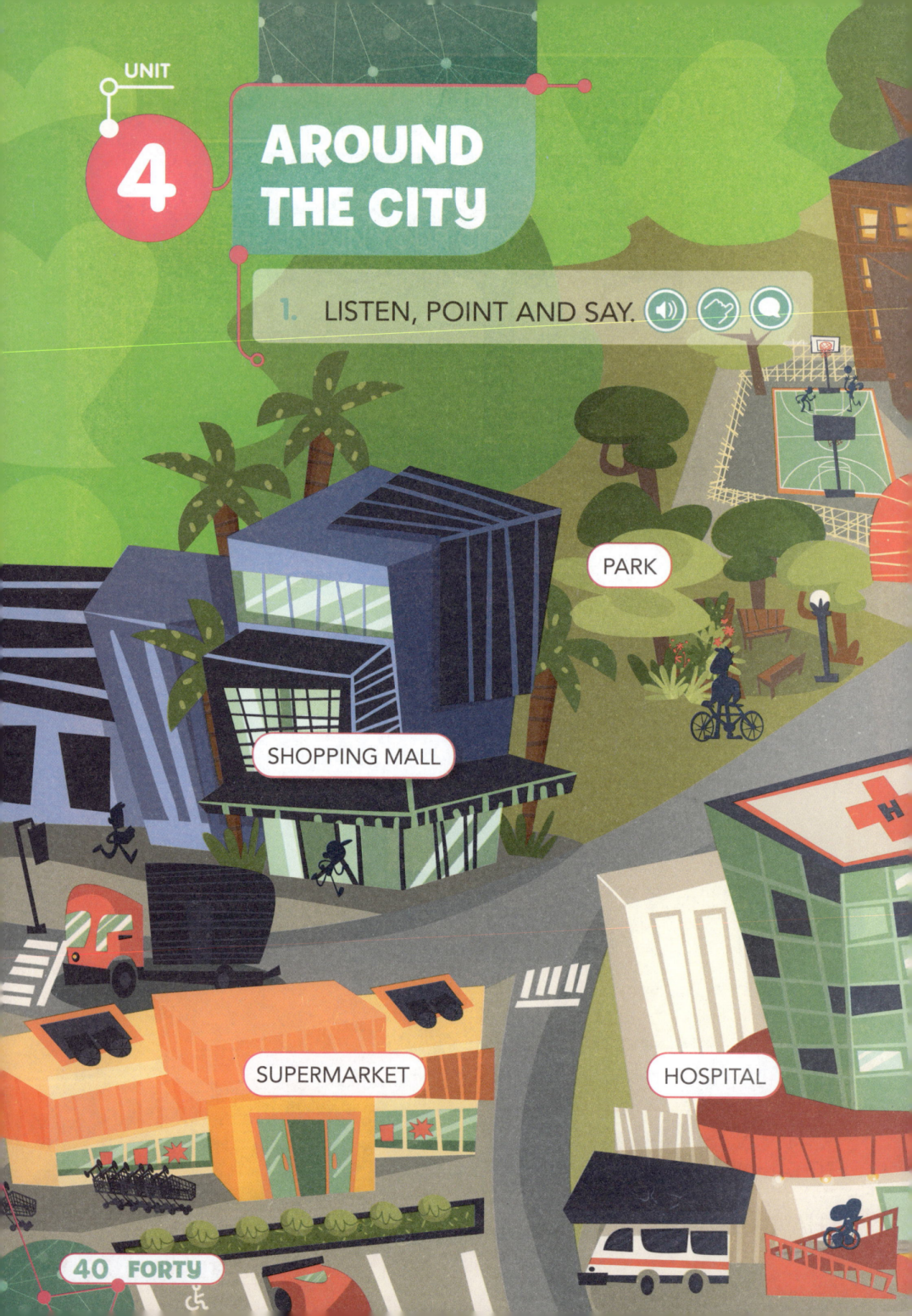

2. LISTEN, STICK AND SAY.

3. LISTEN AND MAKE AN X.

4. LISTEN AND MATCH. WHERE ARE THEY?

5. LISTEN AND WRITE.

MY BALL IS _____
AND _____ .

MY BALL IS _____
AND _____ .

6. COUNT, CIRCLE AND SAY.

7. READ, MAKE AN X AND WRITE.

THE BOYS AND GIRLS ARE AT THE P _____ K.

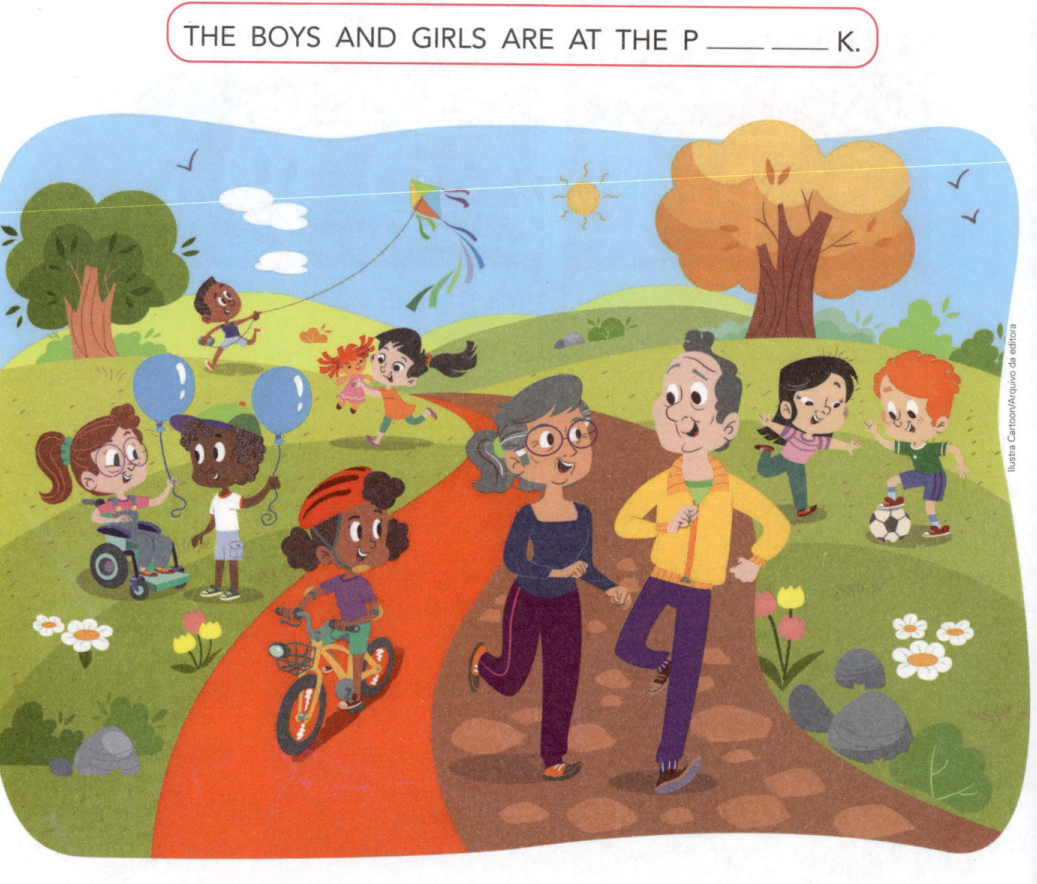

◯ TEACHER	◯ GIRL	◯ BALLOON
◯ KITE	◯ BOOK	◯ BIKE
◯ DOLL	◯ BALL	◯ BOY

8. WRITE THE NAME OF THE PLACES AND MATCH.

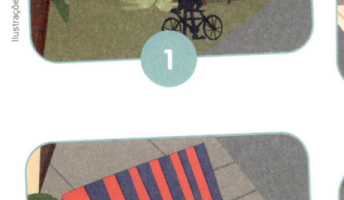

1	P			

2				E		

3	H	O	S				

4		E			S	H	O	

5	S	U			R					T

6				O	O	

LET'S SING!

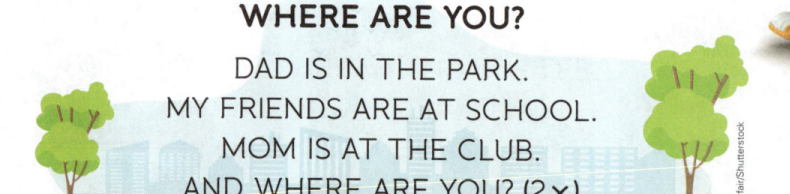

WHERE ARE YOU?

DAD IS IN THE PARK.
MY FRIENDS ARE AT SCHOOL.
MOM IS AT THE CLUB.
AND WHERE ARE YOU? (2x)

9. READ, THINK AND TALK TO A CLASSMATE. WHAT IS YOUR FAVORITE PLACE IN THE CITY?

IT'S THE LOUVRE MUSEUM

Say with Me!

IS THERE A SHARK, IN THE DARK PARK?
IT'S NOT A SHARK, IT'S A ROCK, CLARK!

GROWING UP

RESPECT THE RULES!

10. LOOK AT THE PICTURE AND TALK TO YOUR CLASSMATES.

11. IN GROUPS, TALK ABOUT THE SIGNS. THEN CREATE A POSTER WITH THREE PEDESTRIAN RULES. SHARE IT WITH YOUR CLASSMATES.

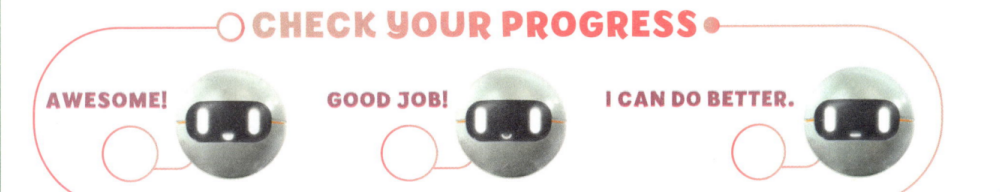

REVIEW

1. READ AND NUMBER.

1. PENCIL	4. SCHOOLBAG	7. PEN
2. NOTEBOOK	5. ERASER	8. PENCIL CASE
3. PENCIL SHARPENER	6. BOOK	9. LUNCH BOX

2. READ AND COMPLETE THE CROSSWORD.

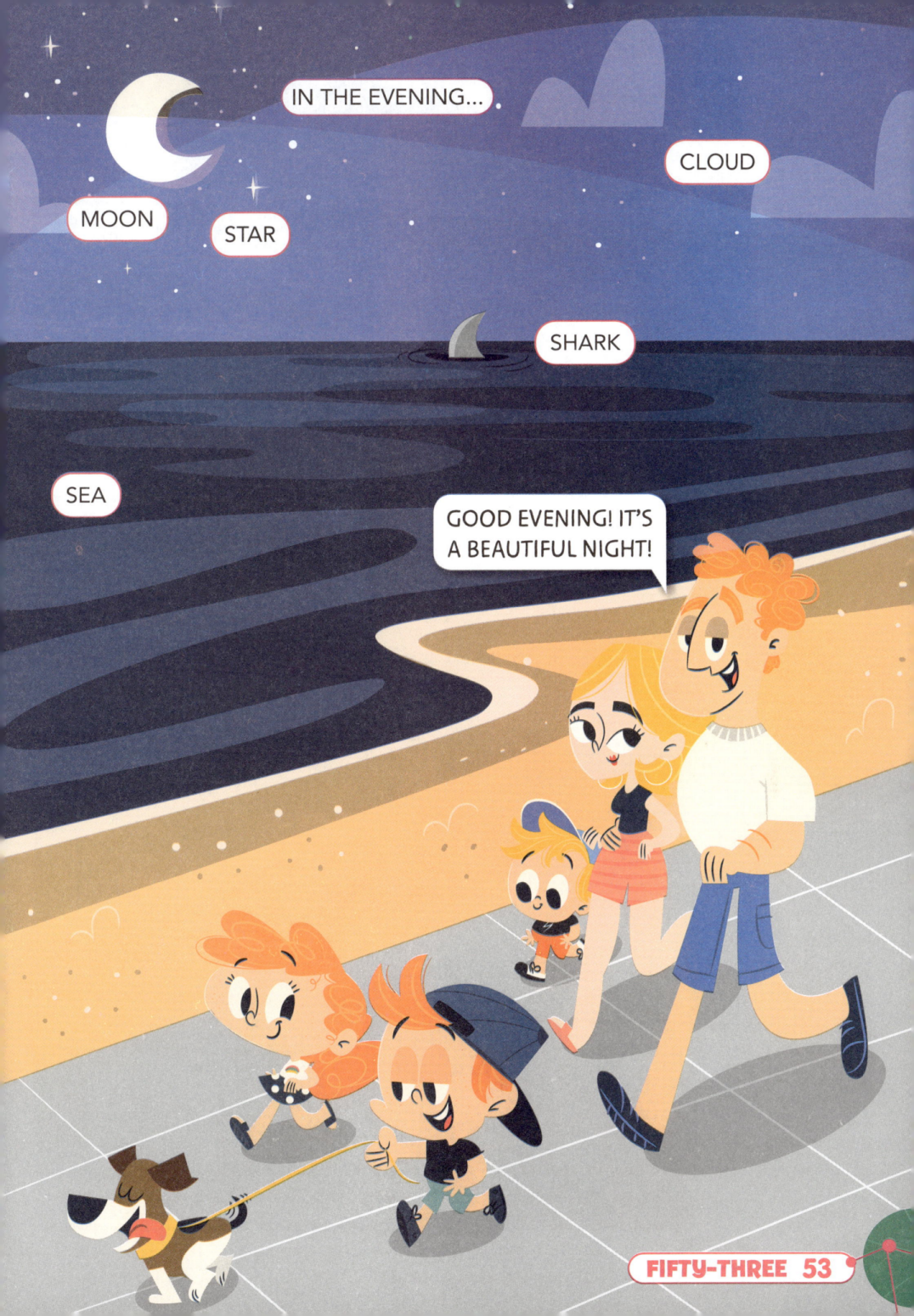

2. LISTEN, STICK AND SAY.

A)

B)

C)

3. LISTEN AND NUMBER.

4. LISTEN, COUNT AND WRITE.

( ) TEN   ( ) ELEVEN   ( ) TWELVE

( ) THIRTEEN   ( ) FOURTEEN   ( ) FIFTEEN

5. COMPLETE THE WORDS.

0   **1**   **2**   **3**   **4**   **5**

Z _ RO   _ NE   TW _   THR _ E   F _ UR   F _ VE

6   **7**   **8**   **9**   **10**   **11**

S _ X   S _ V _ N   E _ GHT   N _ NE   T _ N   _ L _ VEN

12   **13**   **14**   **15**

TW _ LV _   TH _ RT _ EN   F _ URT _ EN   F _ FT _ EN

6. READ AND MAKE AN X.

TODAY IS A BEAUTIFUL DAY AND THE BLAIRS ARE HAVING FUN!

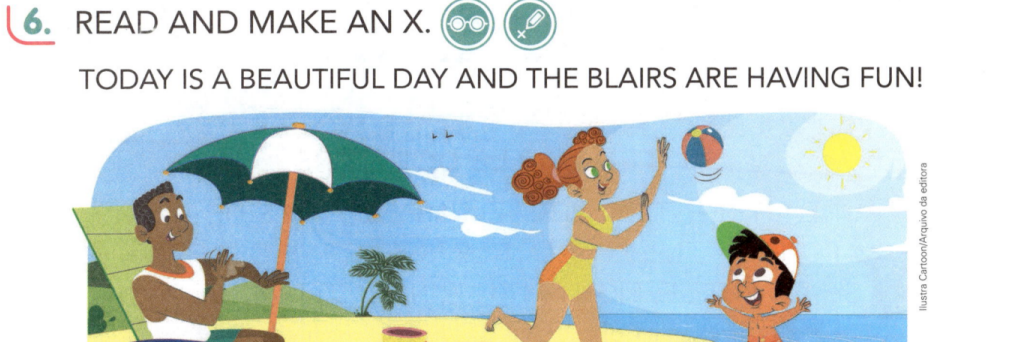

A) IS TODAY A BEAUTIFUL DAY?

○ YES ○ NO

B) WHERE ARE THE BLAIRS TODAY?

○ AT HOME ○ ON THE BEACH

7. COMPLETE THE MISSING LETTERS.

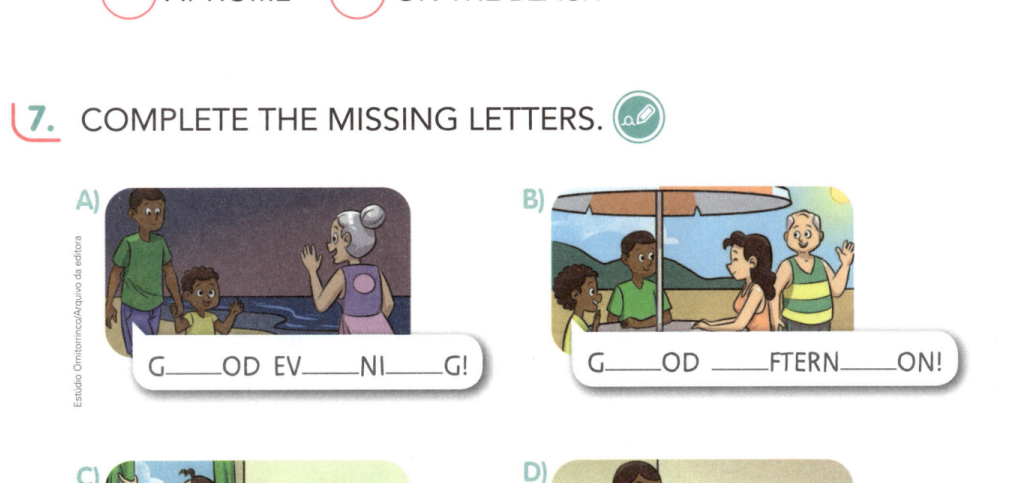

A) G____OD EV____NI____G!

B) G____OD ____FTERN____ON!

C) G____OD M____RNIN____!

D) G____OD N____G____T!

LET'S SING!

TEN LITTLE DOLPHINS

ONE LITTLE, TWO LITTLE, THREE LITTLE DOLPHINS, FOUR LITTLE, FIVE LITTLE, SIX LITTLE DOLPHINS, SEVEN LITTLE, EIGHT LITTLE, NINE LITTLE DOLPHINS, TEN LITTLE BEAUTIFUL DOLPHINS! (2 x)

8. LOOK AN CIRCLE.

A) SHARK / STARFISH

B) FISH / DOLPHIN

C) STARFISH / FISH

D) SHARK / DOLPHIN

Say with Me!

SHE SELLS SEASHELLS ON THE SEASHORE!

GROWING UP

KEEP THE BEACHES CLEAN

9. LOOK AT THE PICTURE AND TALK TO YOUR CLASSMATES.

10. CREATE A POSTER WITH POSSIBLE SOLUTIONS TO AVOID WASTE ON THE BEACHES. SHARE WITH YOUR CLASSMATES.

CHECK YOUR PROGRESS

TIME TO LEARN ABOUT

BEACH SPORTS

WHAT IS YOUR **FAVORITE** BEACH SPORT?

1. LOOK, MATCH AND COLOR.

2. THINK ABOUT YOUR PROTECTION AND CIRCLE.

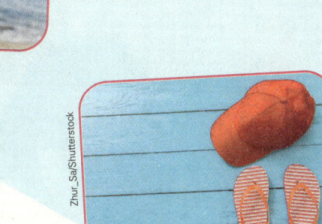

MY FAVORITE BEACH SPORT IS...

3. THINK AND MAKE A COLLAGE.

UNIT 6 I LOVE ANIMALS!

1. LISTEN, POINT AND SAY.

2. LISTEN, STICK AND SAY.

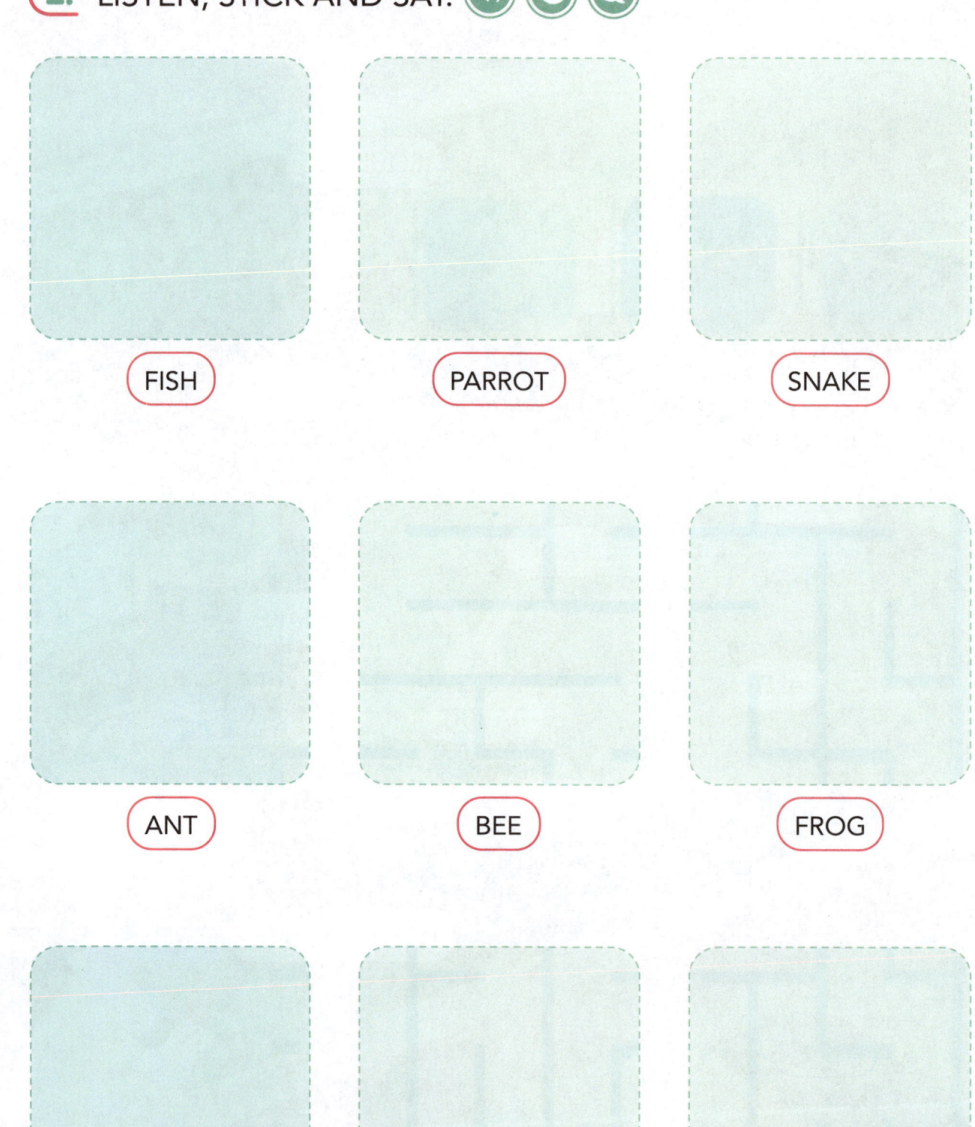

FISH	PARROT	SNAKE
ANT	BEE	FROG
RABBIT	SNAIL	SQUIRREL

3. LISTEN AND CIRCLE **YES** OR **NO**.

4. LISTEN AND COMPLETE.

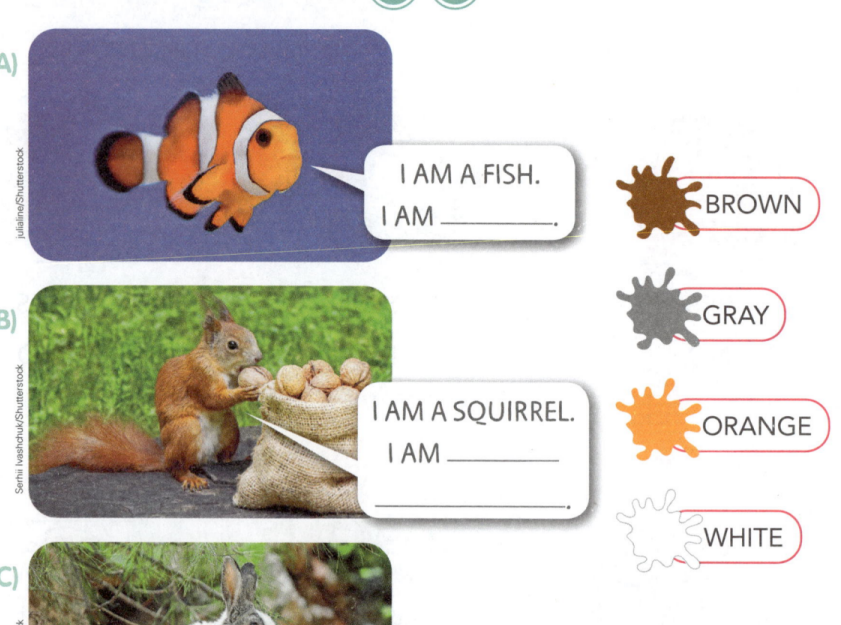

5. LISTEN AND MAKE AN X.

6. READ AND ANSWER.

RABBIT • BEE • PARROT • FISH • FROG • TURTLE

HI, I'M WILLIAM! LOOK AT THE ANIMALS BELOW! THEY'RE SO BEAUTIFUL. MY FAVORITE ANIMAL IS THE FISH. IT IS ORANGE, BLACK AND WHITE.

WHAT IS THIS?

A) IT'S A _____ .

B) IT'S A _____ .

C) IT'S A _____ .

D) IT'S A _____ .

E) IT'S A _____ .

F) IT'S A _____ .

7. COUNT AND WRITE.

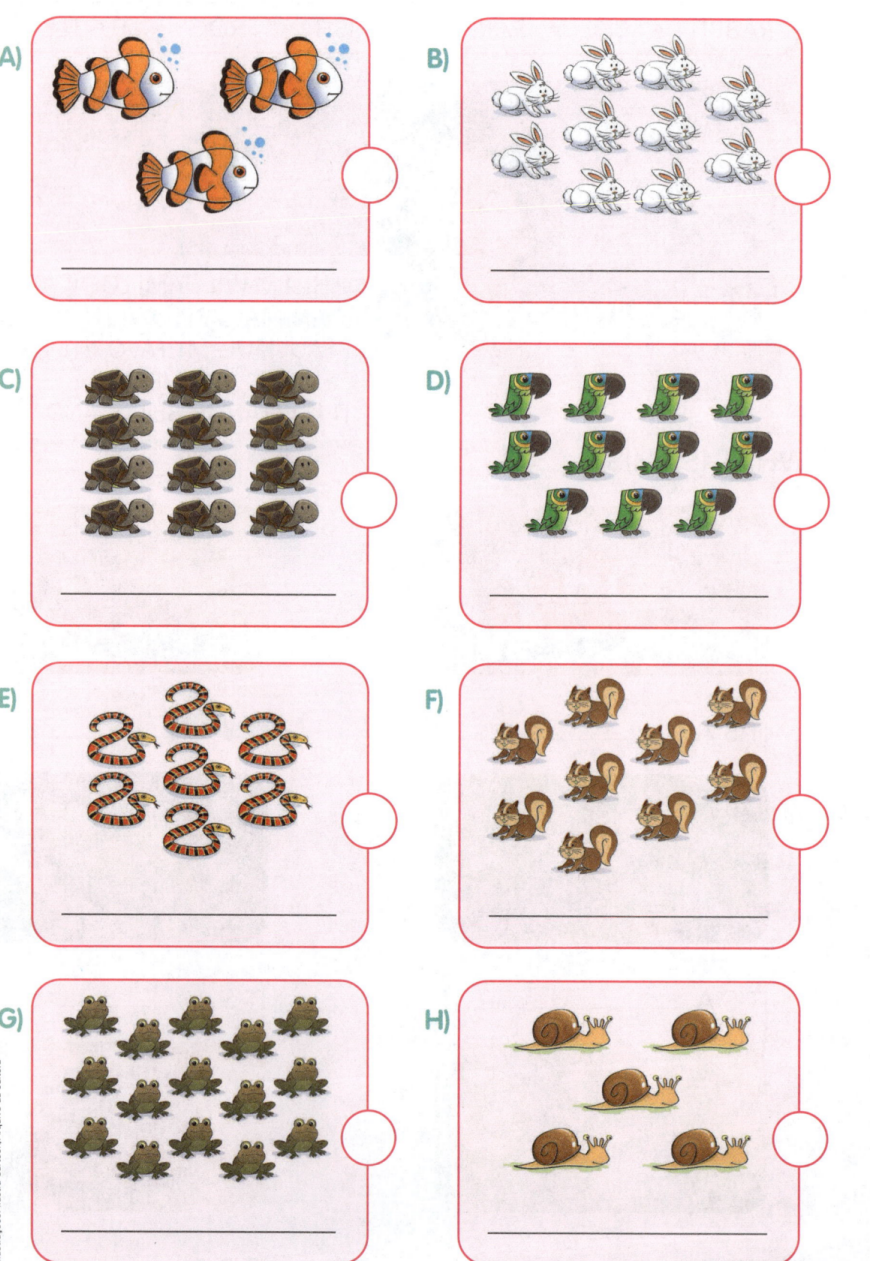

8. FIND IN THE WORDSEARCH AND CIRCLE.

A	A	Z	B	E	E	X	D	C
N	S	N	A	K	E	O	O	A
T	E	L	E	S	H	T	G	T
O	S	P	A	F	R	U	T	H
J	S	Q	U	I	R	R	E	L
D	F	T	E	S	S	T	N	T
V	S	U	G	H	E	L	I	S
F	R	O	G	A	O	E	S	N
J	R	B	M	D	F	W	H	A
Z	T	R	A	B	B	I	T	I
A	P	A	R	R	O	T	E	L

~~ANT~~	FISH	SNAIL
BEE	FROG	SNAKE
CAT	PARROT	SQUIRREL
DOG	RABBIT	TURTLE

LET'S SING!

TWO LITTLE BLACKBIRDS

TWO LITTLE BLACKBIRDS
SITTING ON A HILL.
ONE IS JACK.
THE OTHER IS JILL.
FLY AWAY, JACK.
FLY AWAY, JILL.
COME BACK, JACK.
COME BACK, JILL. (2x)

9. SURVEY. WHAT'S YOUR FAVORITE ANIMAL?

STUDENT'S NAME								

Say with Me!

THE BIG BLACKBIRDS BIT JACK AND JILL SIT ON THE HILL. THE BIG BLACKBIRDS BIT JACK AND JILL SIT ON THE HILL.

GROWING UP

PROTECT THE PARROTS

10. LOOK AT THE PICTURE AND TALK TO YOUR CLASSMATES.

11. DRAW WILD ANIMALS THAT CAN BE CAPTURED FROM THEIR NATURAL HABITAT TO LIVE AWAY FROM NATURE. THEN, CREATE A GROUP COLLECTIVE COLLAGE.

REVIEW

1. COMPLETE THE CROSSWORD.

SHARK • STARFISH • DOLPHIN • FISH • SKY • SANDCASTLE • SEA • MOON • STARS • CLOUD • SEASHELL • SUN

2. CIRCLE AND COMPLETE THE SENTENCES.

A)

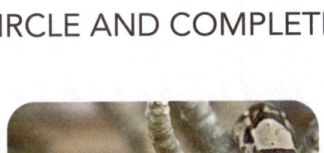

lunatic67/Shutterstock

SNAIL • SNAKE • TURTLE

THE _____ IS IN THE JUNGLE.

B)

Katesalin Pagkaihang/Shutterstock

FISH • FROG • RABBIT

THE _____ IS BLACK AND WHITE.

C)

Tony Moran/Shutterstock

TURTLE • ANT • BEE

THIS IS A _____.

D)

Colin Robert Varndell/Shutterstock

SNAIL • FROG • SQUIRREL

THE _____ IS BEAUTIFUL AND SMALL.

E)

Ondrej Prosicky/Shutterstock

RABBIT • PARROT • FROG

THE _____ IS GREEN.

UNIT 7 TIME FOR BREAKFAST

1. LISTEN, POINT AND SAY.

2. LISTEN, STICK AND SAY.

3. LISTEN AND CIRCLE.

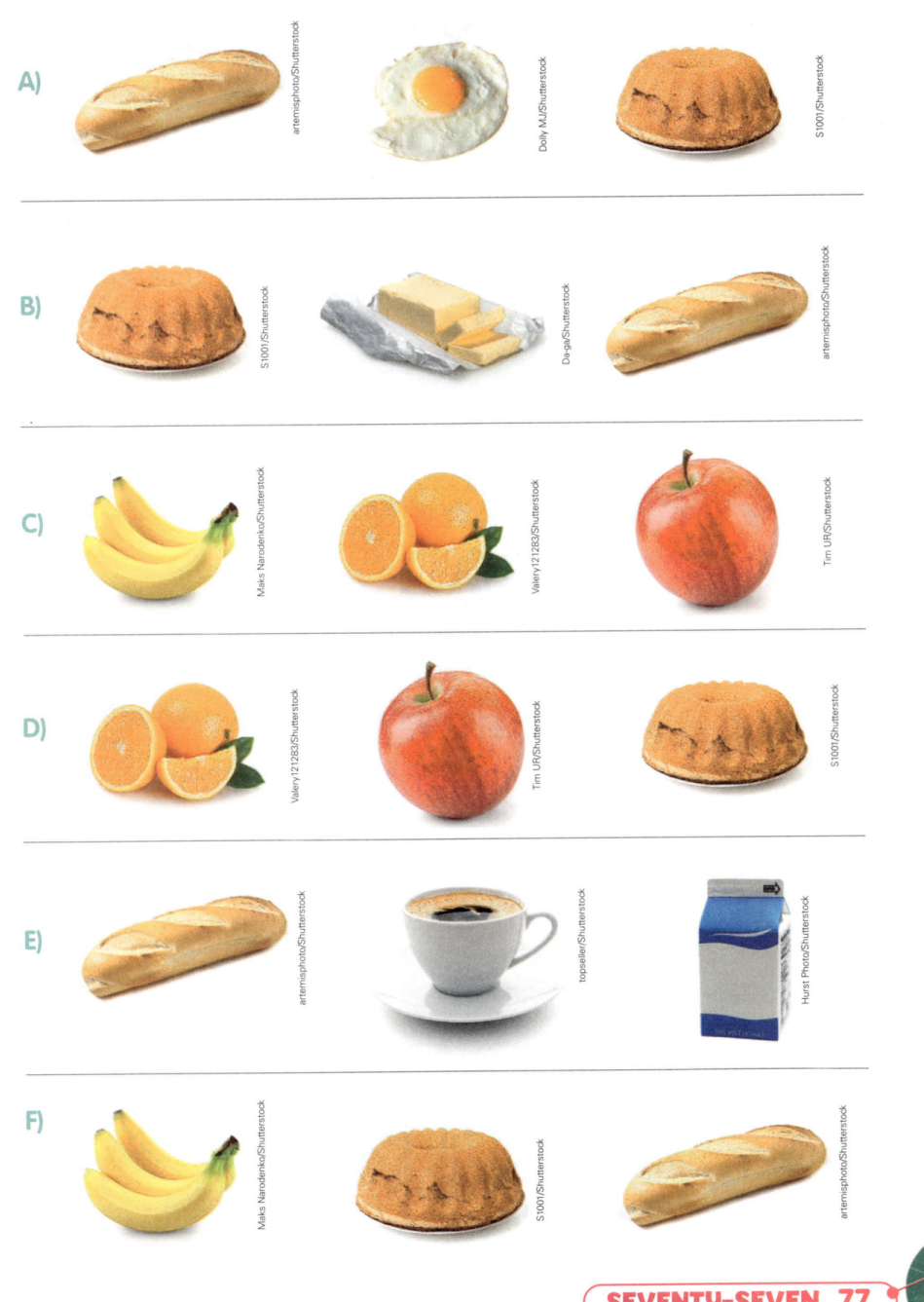

4. LISTEN AND SAY THE NUMBERS. LET'S COUNT.

1	ONE	2	TWO	3	THREE
4	FOUR	5	FIVE	6	SIX
7	SEVEN	8	EIGHT	9	NINE
10	TEN	11	ELEVEN	12	TWELVE
13	THIRTEEN	14	FOURTEEN	15	FIFTEEN
16	SIXTEEN	17	SEVENTEEN	18	EIGHTEEN
19	NINETEEN	20	TWENTY		

5. WRITE THE MISSING NUMBERS AND SAY.

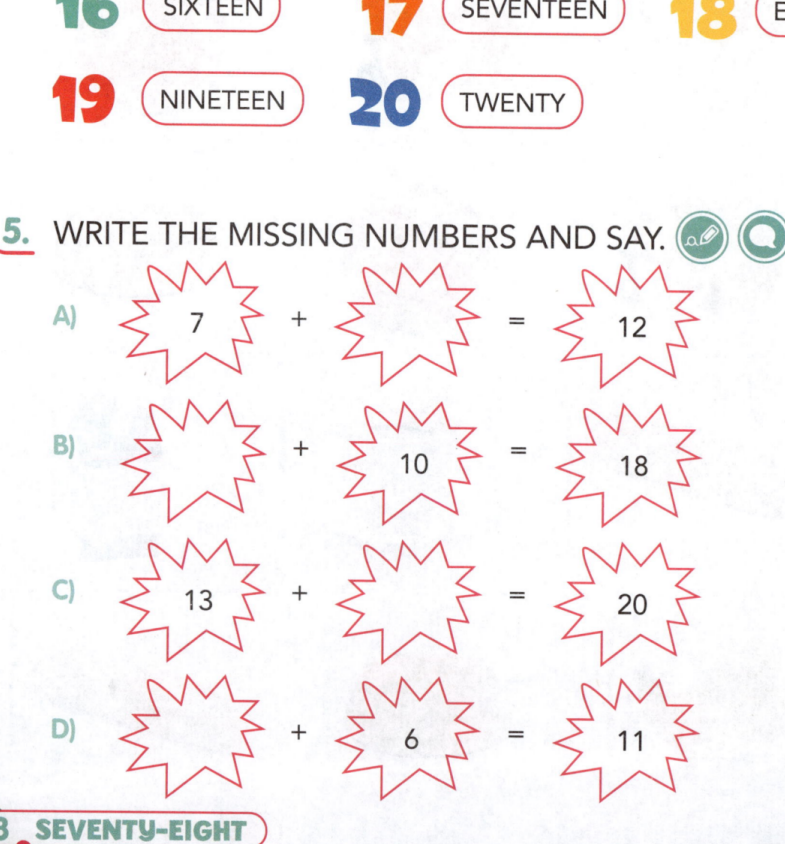

A) 7 + ___ = 12

B) ___ + 10 = 18

C) 13 + ___ = 20

D) ___ + 6 = 11

6. BINGO.

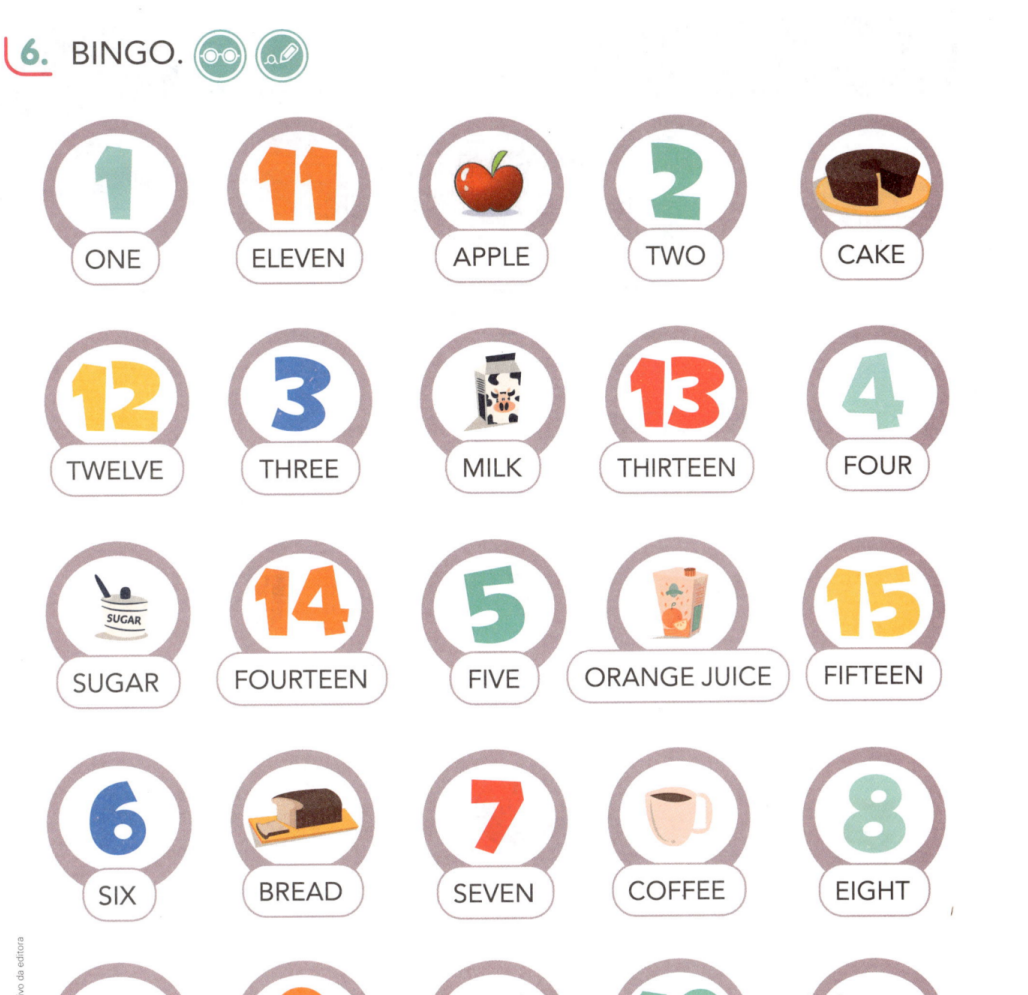

LET'S SING!

HAVE A BREAK!
BREAD AND BUTTER,
COFFEE AND MILK,
COOKIES AND CAKE.
LET'S HAVE A BREAK! (3x)

7. LISTEN AND CIRCLE.

_____

_____

_____

_____

_____

_____

_____

_____

_____

Say with Me!

BREAD AND BUTTER, MILK AND COOKIES;
COOKIES ALL GOODIES.

GROWING UP

EAT HEALTHY FOOD. NO WASTING!

8. LOOK AT THE PICTURE AND TALK TO YOUR CLASSMATES.

9. IN GROUP, TALK ABOUT THE SENTENCES, THEN ANSWER.

DO YOU PREFER TO EAT HEALTHY FOOD EVERY DAY?

○ YES.　　○ NO.

DO YOU WASTE ANY FOOD?

○ YES.　　○ NO.

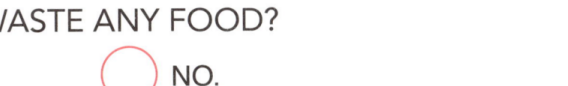

TIME TO LEARN ABOUT THE FOOD WE EAT

1. LOOK, THINK AND MATCH.

WHERE DOES THE FOOD COME FROM?

2. IN PAIRS, COMPLETE THE CHART USING THE WORDS FROM THE BOX. WHERE DO FRUITS AND VEGETABLES GROW?

AVOCADO • APPLE • BEETS • BLUEBERRY • CARROTS • CHERRY • GARLIC • LIME • ONION • ORANGE • PEACH • PEAR • POTATO • RADISH • RASPBERRY • RED PEPPER • STRAWBERRY • TOMATO

	UNDER THE SOIL:
	ON A BUSH:
	ON A TREE:

THE BEANS IN MY PLATE COME FROM...

3. LOOK AT THE GERMINATION IN THE SOIL AND NUMBER. THEN PLANT YOUR OWN BEAN.

2. LISTEN, STICK AND SAY.

THE HUMAN BODY!

3. LISTEN AND CIRCLE.

4. LISTEN AND ANSWER.

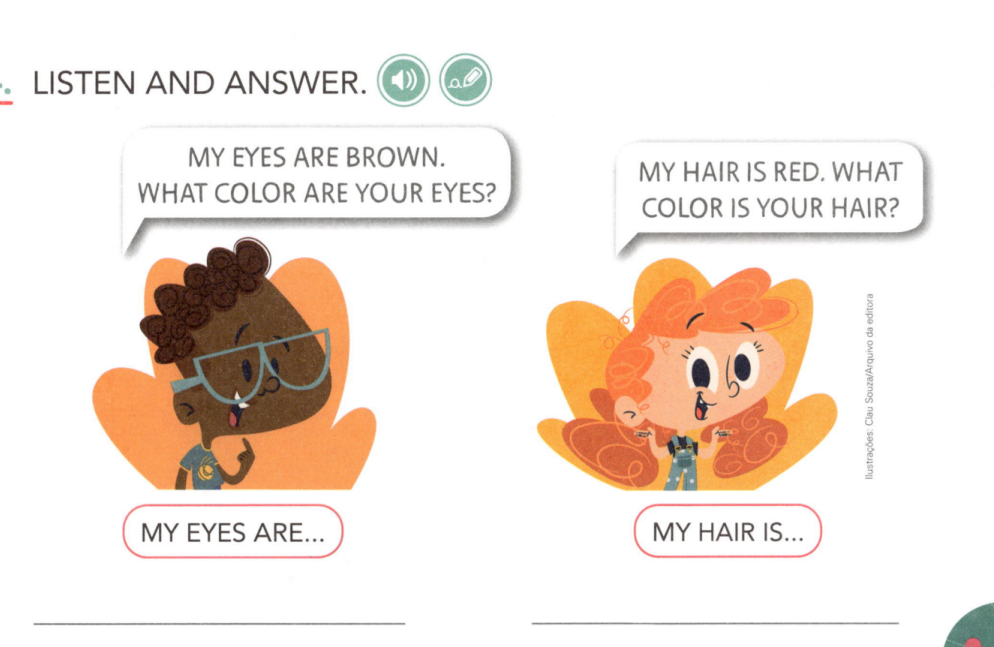

5. READ AND COMPLETE.

BLACK • BLUE • EYES • BROWN • HAIR • RED

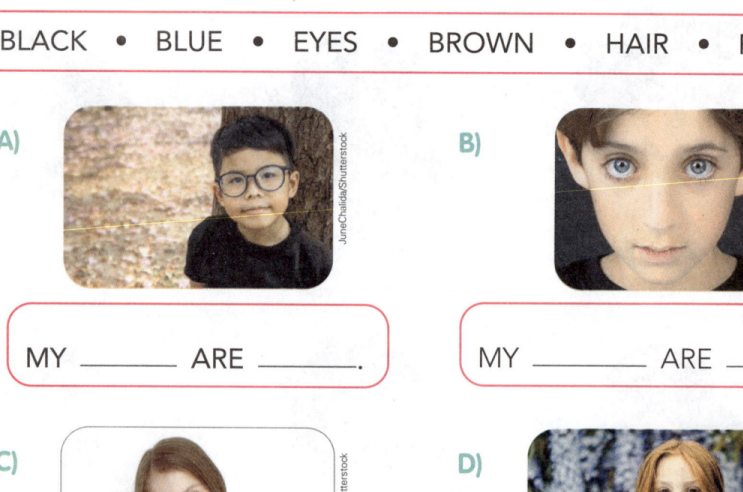

A)

MY _____ ARE _____.

B)

MY _____ ARE _____.

C)

MY _____ IS _____.

D)

MY _____ IS _____.

6. READ AND MATCH.

LOOK AT THIS GIRL!
SHE IS AMÉLIE.
HER HAIR IS DARK BROWN.
HER EYES ARE DARK BROWN.
SHE IS FROM FRANCE.

EAR

EYE

NOSE

MOUTH

7. WRITE. COMPLETE THE CROSSWORD.

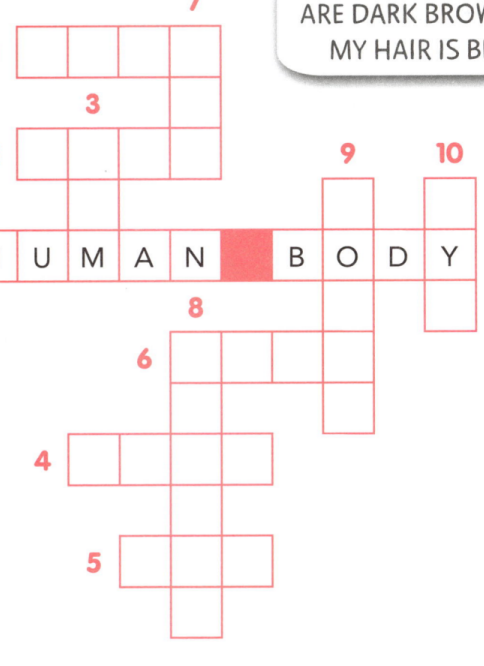

NOW YOU!

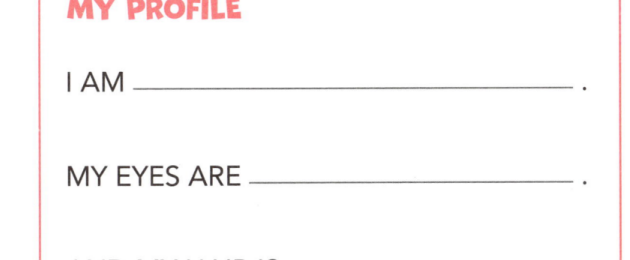

8. WRITE, COMPLETE AND COLOR THE ROBOT.

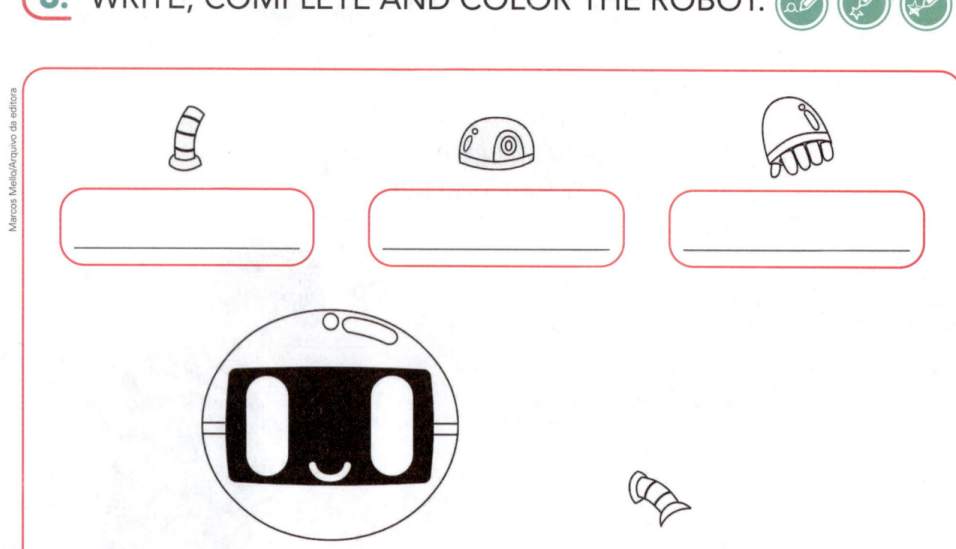

9. COLOR, DRAW AND WRITE.

10. LOOK AND DRAW YOUR OWN AVATAR.

LET'S SING!

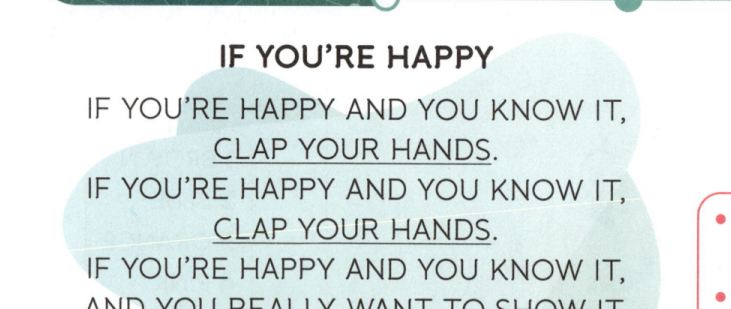

IF YOU'RE HAPPY

IF YOU'RE HAPPY AND YOU KNOW IT,
CLAP YOUR HANDS.
IF YOU'RE HAPPY AND YOU KNOW IT,
CLAP YOUR HANDS.
IF YOU'RE HAPPY AND YOU KNOW IT,
AND YOU REALLY WANT TO SHOW IT,
IF YOU'RE HAPPY AND YOU KNOW IT,
CLAP YOUR HANDS.

- SNAP YOU FINGERS.
- STAMP YOUR FEET.
- DO ALL THREE.

11. MATCH.

A) • SNAP YOUR FINGERS.

B) • STAMP YOUR FEET.

C) • CLAP YOUR HANDS.

Say with Me!

LITTLE JOHNNY WASHES HIS FEET BEFORE GOING TO SLEEP. DO YOU WASH YOUR FEET BEFORE GOING TO SLEEP?

GROWING UP

TAKE CARE OF YOUR BODY

12. LOOK AT THE PICTURE AND TALK TO YOUR CLASSMATES.

13. IN GROUPS, CHOOSE THREE ACTIONS ABOUT TAKING CARE OF YOUR BODY. DRAW AND COLOR THEM.

CHECK YOUR PROGRESS

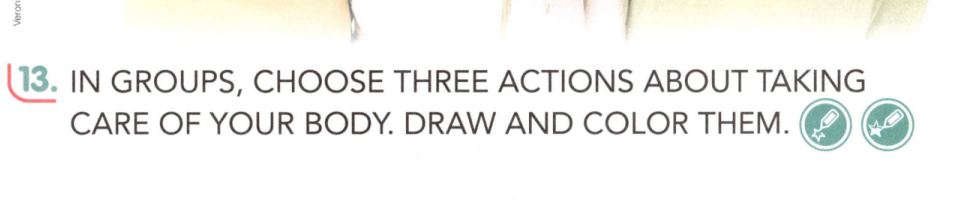

REVIEW

1. CIRCLE AND WRITE.

WHAT DO YOU LIKE?

A)	BANANAS		APPLES
B)	ORANGE		PAPAYA
C)	ORANGE JUICE		COFFEE
D)	CAKE		BREAD AND BUTTER
E)	EGG		MILK

I LIKE _____ , _____ , _____ ,

_____ , _____ , _____ .

2. FIND AND WRITE THE WORDS.

ARM • FOOT • EAR • HAIR • MOUTH •
EYE • LEG • FINGER • NOSE • HAND

A	U	T	C	I	R	C	O	V	Q	C	A	R	M
A	E	A	R	C	Y	H	A	N	D	O	H	C	P
M	Y	F	J	I	P	O	T	Z	O	P	U	E	C
W	O	F	B	M	N	O	P	A	I	B	Q	P	S
X	A	C	B	N	O	U	L	E	G	T	M	O	F
E	T	H	B	Y	S	N	I	T	Y	I	O	T	I
Y	L	A	T	J	E	F	K	L	R	E	U	A	N
E	R	I	Z	F	L	O	U	B	C	M	T	U	G
B	E	R	A	L	N	F	O	O	T	E	H	P	E
A	P	C	E	T	L	P	C	E	J	O	L	I	R

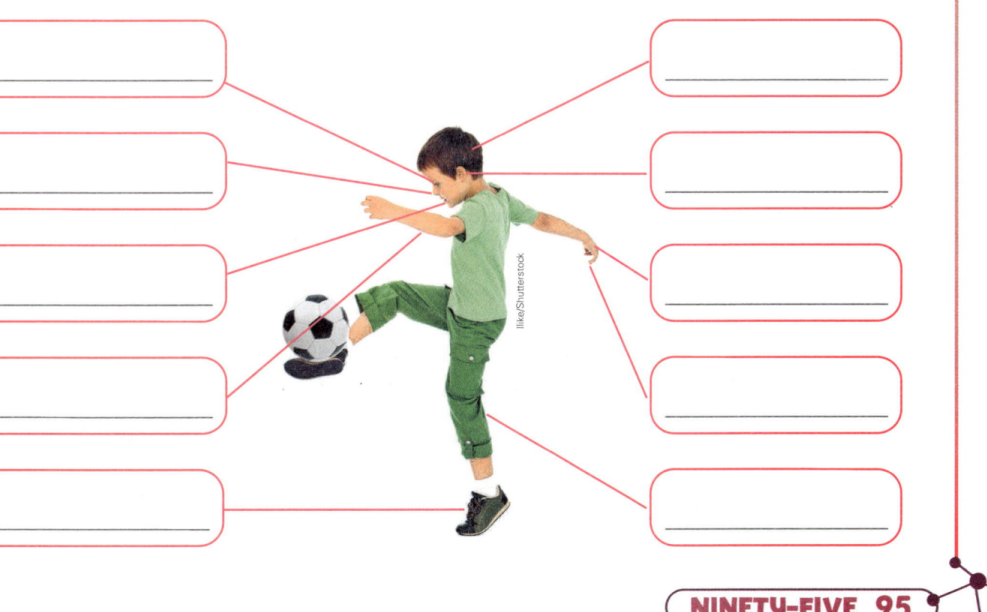

EXTRA PRACTICE 1

1. MATCH.

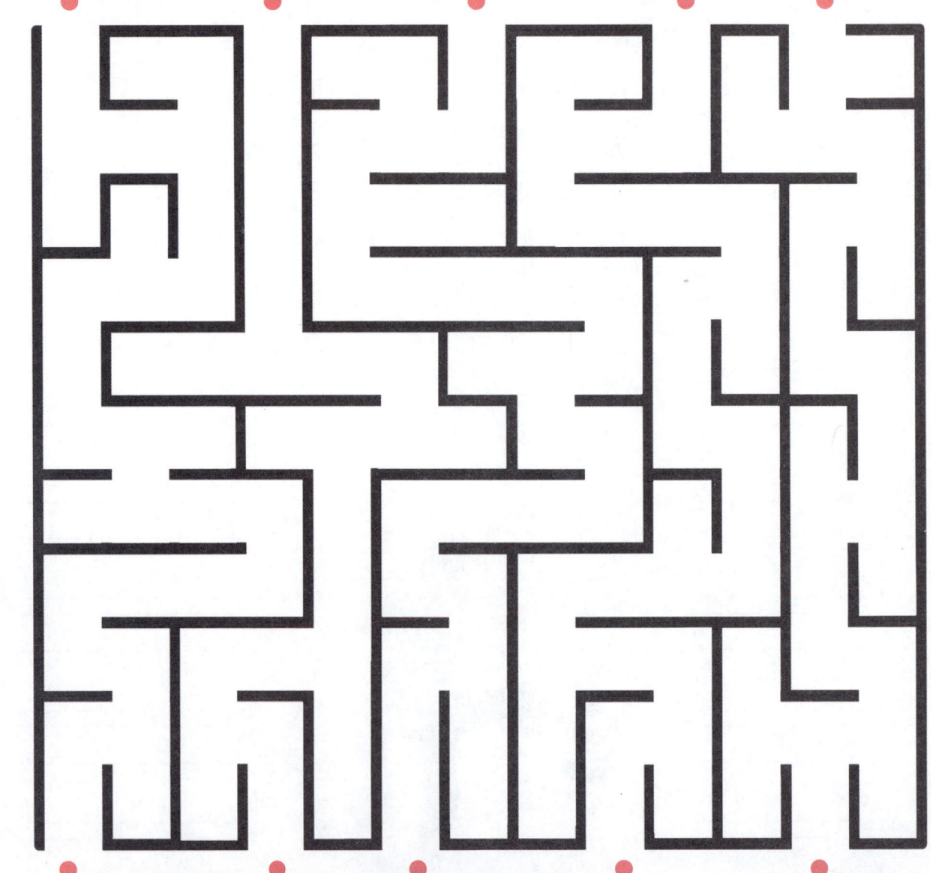

EXTRA PRACTICE 2

1. MAKE AN X IN THE CORRECT ALTERNATIVE AND COLOR THE PICTURE.

THIS HOUSE HAS...

A) ⃝ TWO BEDROOMS, TWO BATHROOMS AND A LIVING ROOM.

B) ⃝ TWO BEDROOMS, ONE BATHROOM, A LIVING ROOM, A KITCHEN AND A LAUNDRY ROOM.

C) ⃝ TWO BEDROOMS, ONE BATHROOM, A LIVING ROOM AND A KITCHEN.

D) ⃝ TWO BEDROOMS, TWO BATHROOMS, A GARDEN AND A GARAGE.

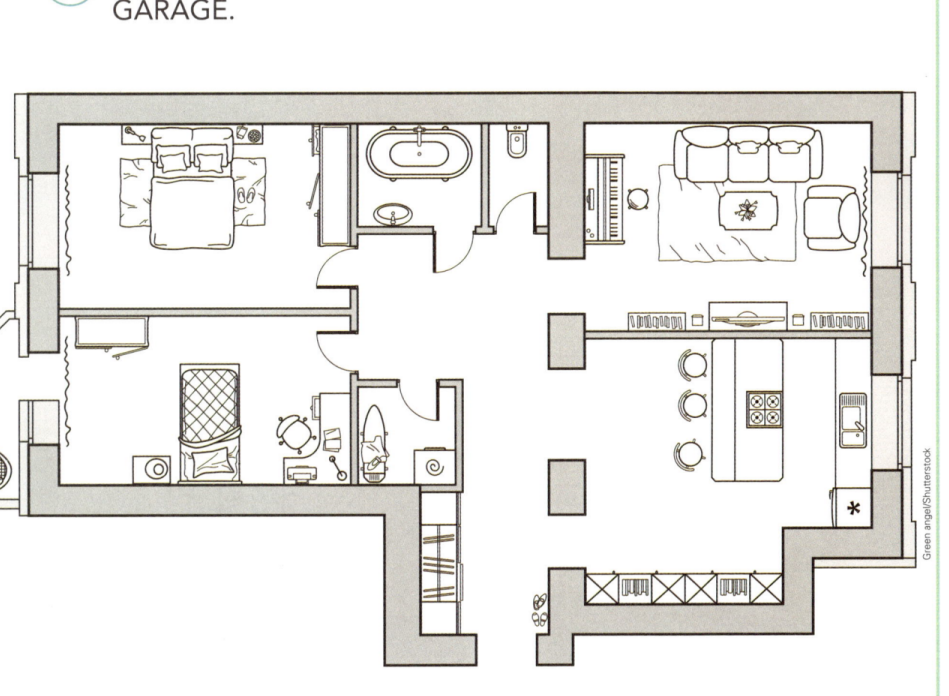

EXTRA PRACTICE 3

1. MATCH AND COMPLETE.

FIVE • SEVEN • THREE • EIGHT • TWO

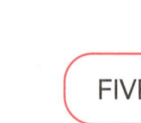 ___ W ___ •   •

 ___ ___ GH ___ •   •

 ___ I ___ E •   •

 ___ HRE ___ •   •

 S ___ ___ EN •   •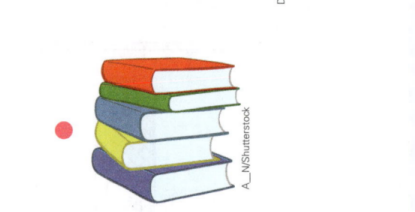

EXTRA PRACTICE 4

1. FIND AND CIRCLE.

D3	A BABY • A GIRL • A BOY • A BALL • A BIKE
E2	A BABY • A GIRL • A BOY • A BALL • A BIKE
A1	A BABY • A GIRL • A BOY • A BALL • A BIKE
E4	A BABY • A GIRL • A BOY • A BALL • A BIKE
B3	A BABY • A GIRL • A BOY • A BALL • A BIKE

EXTRA PRACTICE 5

1. READ, DRAW AND COLOR.

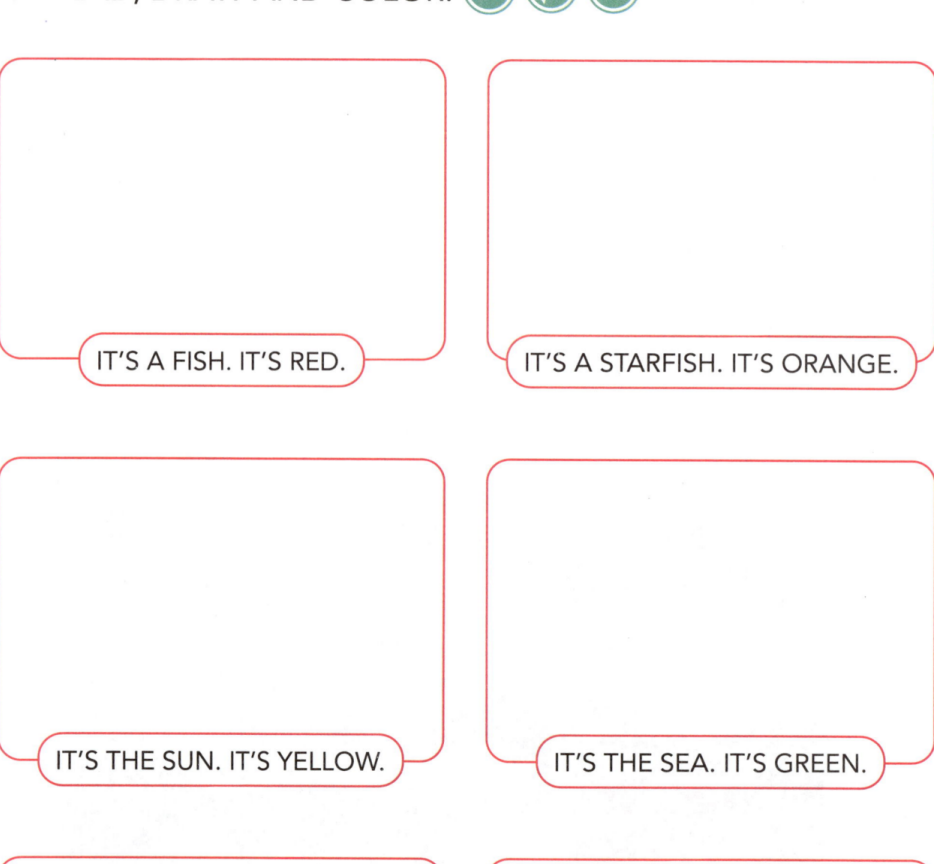

IT'S A FISH. IT'S RED.

IT'S A STARFISH. IT'S ORANGE.

IT'S THE SUN. IT'S YELLOW.

IT'S THE SEA. IT'S GREEN.

IT'S A SEASHELL. IT'S BLUE.

IT'S A SANDCASTLE. IT'S BROWN.

EXTRA PRACTICE 6

1. COMPLETE THE CROSSWORD.

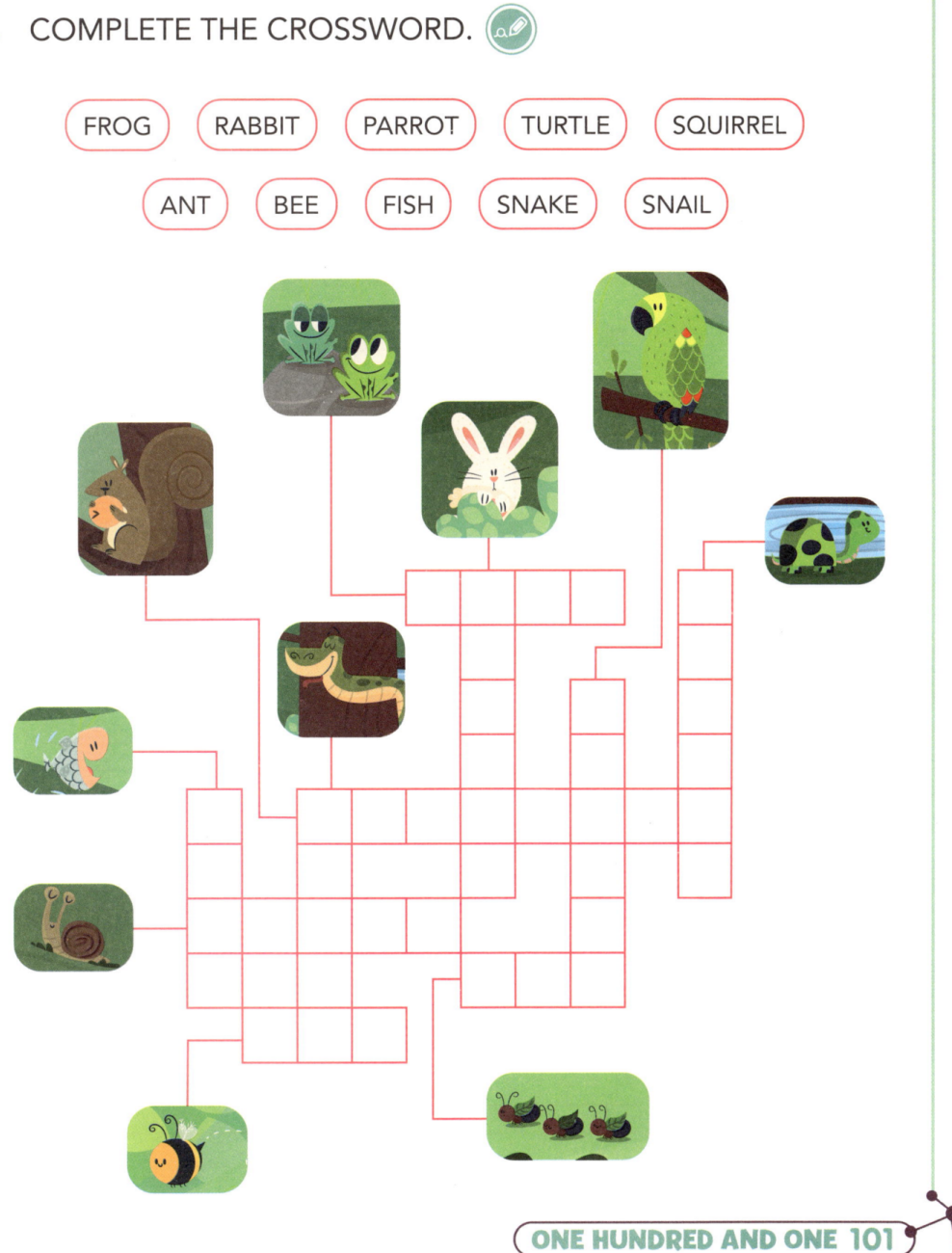

EXTRA PRACTICE 7

1. WRITE ACCORDING TO THE SYMBOLS.

✏	@	✂	♦	✍	△	🏛	☎	✖	✉	🖥	🏧	➜	🎅	👤	❄	✿	⚙	☆
A	B	C	D	E	F	G	I	K	L	M	N	O	P	R	S	T	U

(A) ✍ + 🏛 + 🏛 + ✿ = ___

(B) ✂ + ✏ + ✖ + ✍ = ___

(C) 🖥 + ☎ + ✉ + ✖ = ___

(D) @ + 👤 + ✍ + ✏ + ♦ = ___

(E) ✿ + ☆ + 🏛 + ✏ + 👤 = ___

(F) ✂ + ➜ + △ + △ + ✍ + ✍ = ___

(G) ✏ + 🎅 + 🎅 + ✉ + ✍ + ✿ = ___

(H) @ + ☆ + ⚙ + ⚙ + ✍ + 👤 = ___

(I) @ + ✏ + 🏧 + ✏ + 🏧 + ✏ + ✿ = ___

EXTRA PRACTICE 8

1. READ THE INFORMATION FROM THE BOX AND DRAW YOUR MONSTER. THEN COLOR IT.

3 LEGS	**5** EYES	**1** MOUTH	**8** FINGERS
6 ARMS	**2** NOSES	**4** EARS	**10** TOES

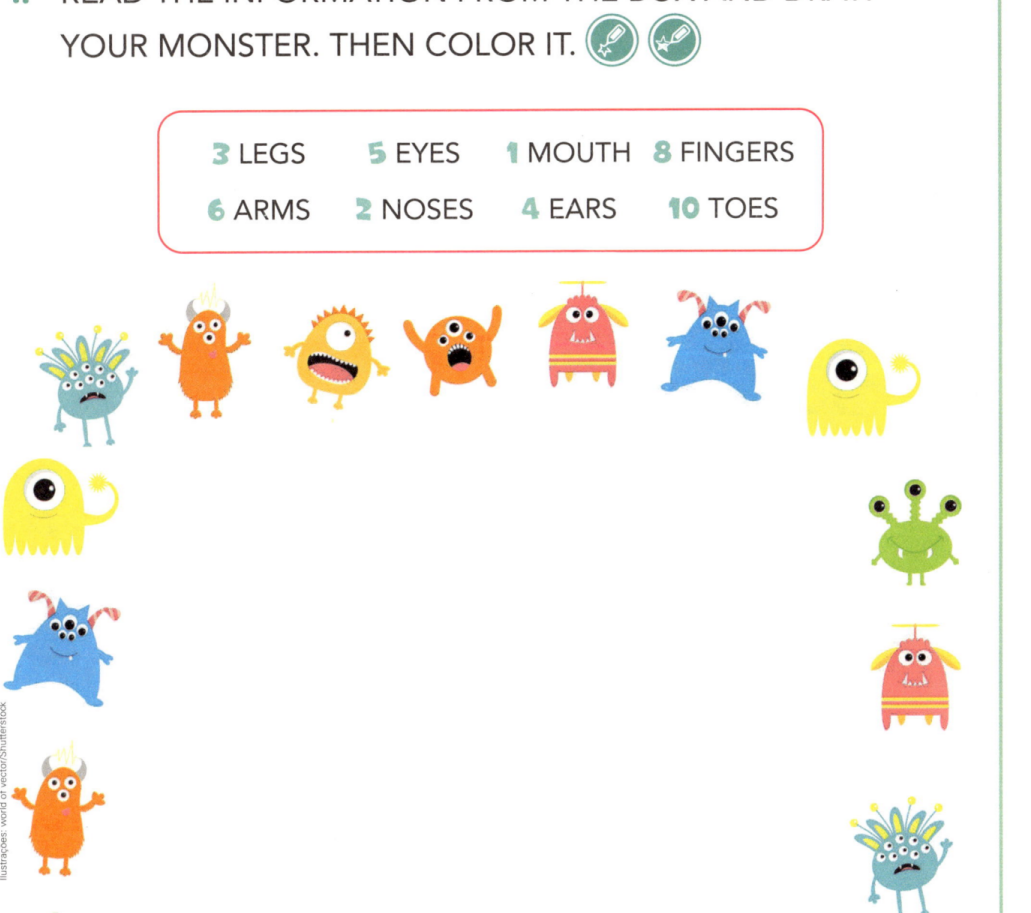

PROJECT 1 URBAN OR RURAL?

1. LOOK AT THE PICTURES AND CHECK THE PLACES THAT CAN BE FOUND IN YOUR CITY. ✓

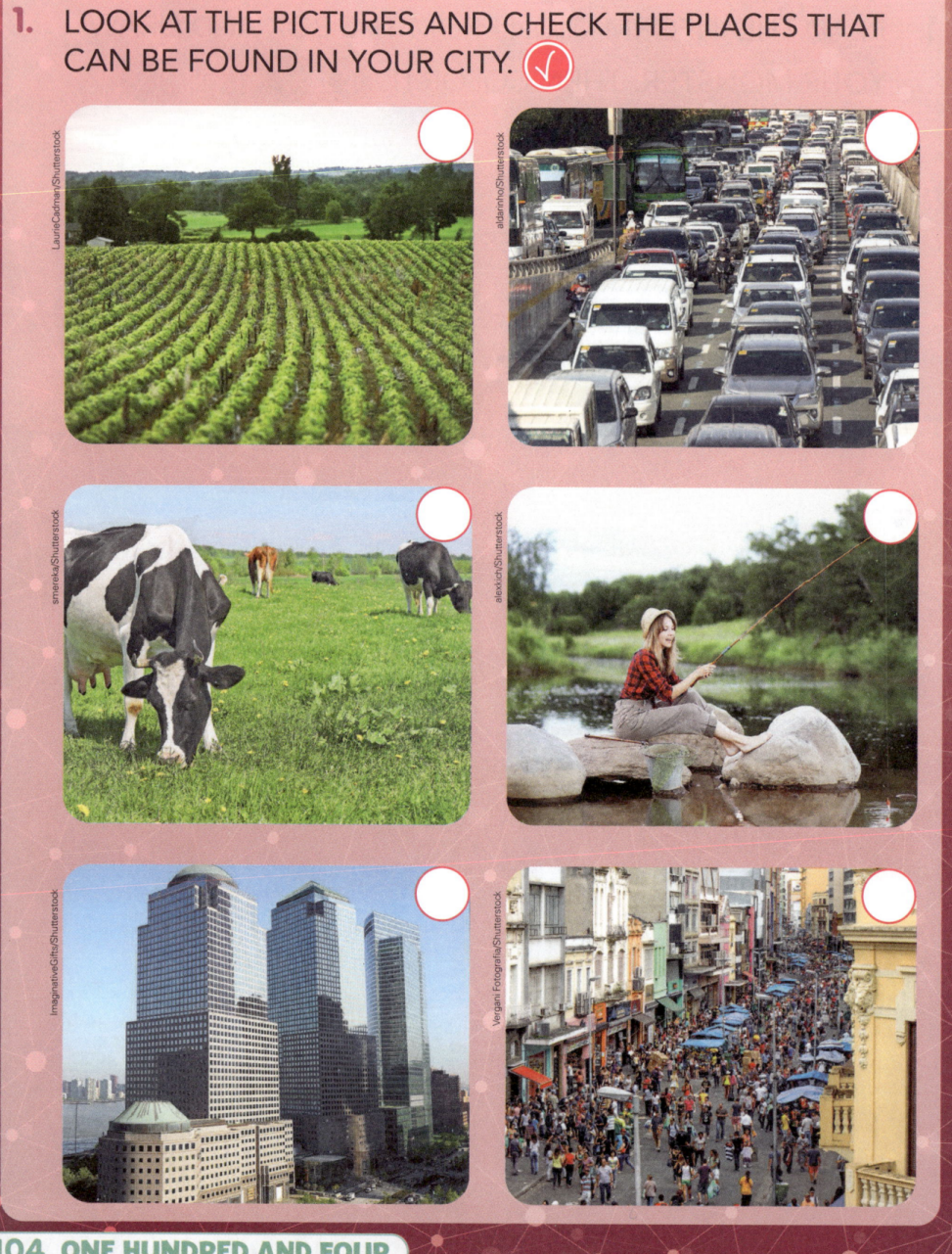

2. WRITE URBAN OR RURAL. THEN PLAY A GUESSING GAME.

3. CHOOSE A CITY AND FIND INFORMATION ABOUT IT.

4. SHOW YOUR RESEARCH TO YOUR CLASSMATES AND PARTICIPATE IN A COMMUNITY GALLERY!

PROJECT 2 ONE FISH, TWO FISH...

1. LOOK AND WRITE THE FISH PARTS.

SCALES • HEAD • MOUTH • TAIL • FIN • EYE

_ E A _

E _ E

M _ U _ _

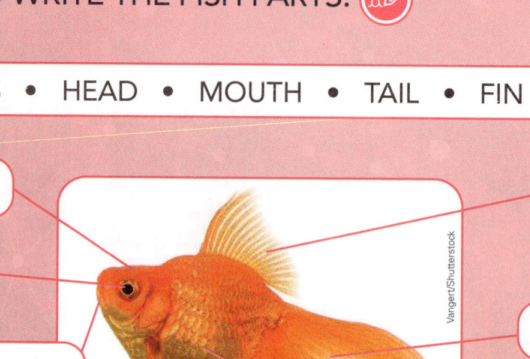

F _ _ _

_ A _ L

S _ _ L _ S

2. PLAY THE GUESS GAME. WHAT FISH IS IT?

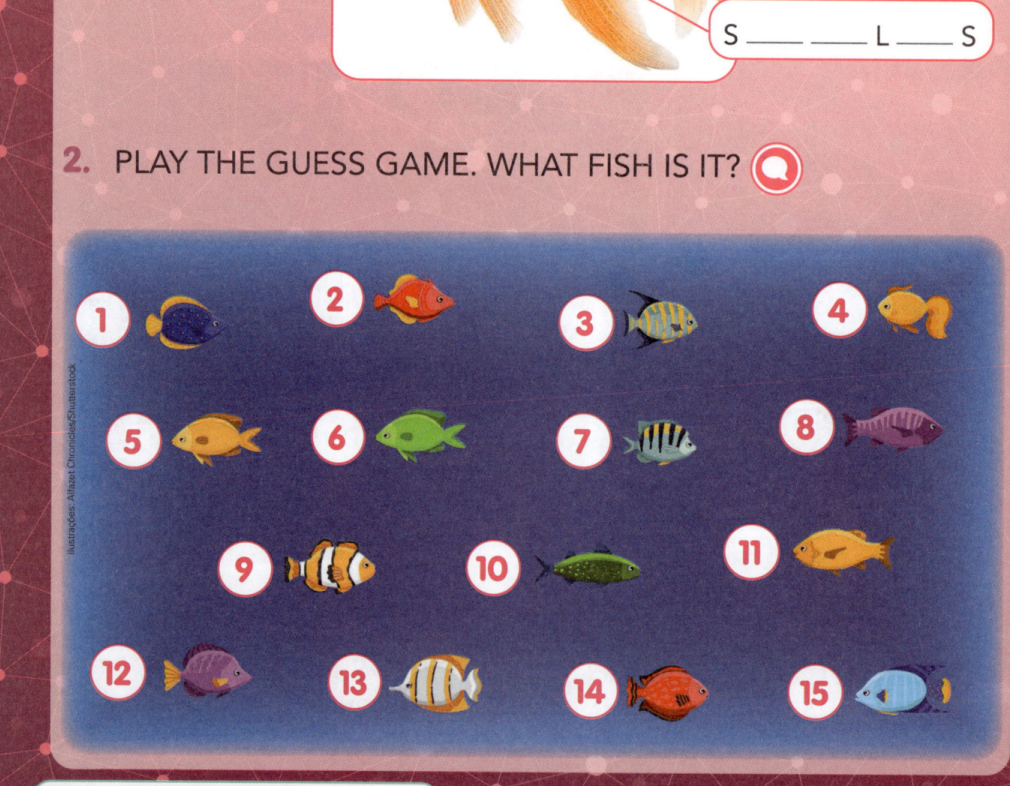

3. LOOK AT THE PICTURES OF OTHER SEA ANIMALS. WHAT ARE THEIR NAMES? CIRCLE THE CORRECT WORDS.

SEAHORSE

SEA TURTLE

STARFISH

STINGRAY

STARFISH

SEA TURTLE

STARFISH

STINGRAY

4. DO SOME RESEARCH AND FIND OTHER KINDS OF FISH OR SEA ANIMALS AND THEIR NAMES IN ENGLISH.

5. SHARE YOUR RESEARCH WITH YOUR CLASSMATES AND COLLABORATE TO THE SEA DISPLAY!

GLOSSARY

A

A: UM(A)

AM: SOU; ESTOU

AN: UM(A)

AND: E

ANSWER: RESPONDER; RESPOSTA

ANT: FORMIGA

ANT HILL: FORMIGUEIRO

APPLE: MAÇÃ

ARE: SÃO; ESTÃO

ARM: BRAÇO

AROUND: PELO(A)

AVOCADO: ABACATE

B

BABY BROTHER: IRMÃO MENOR

BALL: BOLA

BALLOON: BEXIGA; BALÃO

BATHROOM: BANHEIRO

BE A GOOD LISTENER: SEJA UM BOM OUVINTE

BE CAREFUL: TOME CUIDADO

BE KIND: SEJA GENEROSO

BE POSITIVE: SEJA POSITIVO

BEACH: PRAIA

BEACH SAND: AREIA DA PRAIA

BEACH SOCCER: FUTEBOL DE PRAIA

BEACH SPORTS: ESPORTES DE PRAIA

BEACH VOLLEY: VÔLEI DE PRAIA

BEANS: FEIJÃO

BEAUTIFUL: BONITO(A)

BED: CAMA

BEDROOM: QUARTO

BEE: ABELHA

BEEHIVE: COLMEIA

BEET: BETERRABA

BIG: GRANDE

BIKE: BICICLETA

BIRD: PÁSSARO

BIRTHDAY: ANIVERSÁRIO

BIT: MORDER

BLACK: PRETO

BLUE: AZUL

BLUEBERRY: MIRTILO

BOARD GAME: JOGO DE TABULEIRO

BODY: CORPO

BOOK: LIVRO

BOY: MENINO

BREAD: PÃO

BREAK: RECREIO; PAUSA PARA O LANCHE

BREAKFAST: CAFÉ DA MANHÃ

BROTHER: IRMÃO

BROWN: MARROM

BUILDING BLOCKS: BLOQUINHOS DE MONTAR

BUS: ÔNIBUS

BUSH: ARBUSTO

BUTTER: MANTEIGA

C

CAKE: BOLO

CAN: PODER

CAP: BONÉ

CAPTURED: CAPTURADO

CARD: CARTÃO

CARROT: CENOURA

CAT: GATO

CHANT: CANTO RITMADO

CHARACTER: PERSONAGEM

CHART: TABELA, QUADRO

CHERRY: CEREJA

CHESS: XADREZ

CHOCOLATE MILK: ACHOCOLATADO

CHOPPED: PICADO

CITY: CIDADE

CLAP: BATER PALMAS

CLASSROOM: SALA DE AULA

CLEAN: LIMPO(A)

CLOUD: NUVEM

COFFEE: CAFÉ

COLLABORATIVE: COLABORATIVO

COLLAGE: COLAGEM

COLOR: COLORIR; COR

COMPLETE: COMPLETAR

COOKIE: BISCOITO; BOLACHA

COOPERATION: COOPERAÇÃO

COSTUME: FANTASIA

COUNT: CONTAR

COUNTRY: CAMPO; ZONA RURAL

CROSSWALK: FAIXA DE PEDESTRES

CROSSWORD: PALAVRAS CRUZADAS

CUT: CORTAR

D

DAD: PAPAI

DARK: ESCURO

DATE: DATA
DAY: DIA
DEAR: QUERIDO(A)
DIFFERENCE: DIFERENÇA
DINOSAUR(S): DINOSSAURO(S)
DO: FAZER
DO YOUR BEST: FAÇA O SEU MELHOR
DOG: CACHORRO
DOLL: BONECA
DOLPHIN: GOLFINHO
DRAW: DESENHAR
DRAWING: DESENHO

E

EACH: CADA
EAR: ORELHA
EAT: COMER
EGG: OVO
EGG RACE: CORRIDA DOS OVOS

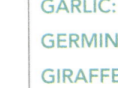

ERASER: BORRACHA
EXHIBITION: EXPOSIÇÃO
EYE: OLHO

F

FACE: ROSTO
FEET: PÉS
FIDGET TOY: BRINQUEDO ANTIESTRESSE
FIFTEEN: QUINZE
FIN: NADADEIRA, BARBATANA
FIND: ENCONTRAR
FINGER: DEDO DA MÃO
FINISH: FIM
FISH: PEIXE(S)
FLOWER: FLOR
FOOT: PÉ

FOOTVOLLEY: FUTEVÔLEI
FRIEND: AMIGO(A)
FRIENDSHIP: AMIZADE

FROG: SAPO
FRUIT: FRUTA

G

GAME: JOGO
GARAGE: GARAGEM
GARDEN: JARDIM
GARLIC: ALHO
GERMINATION: GERMINAÇÃO
GIRAFFE: GIRAFA
GIRL: MENINA
GLASS: COPO
GLUE: COLAR; COLA
GO: IR
GO AHEAD: ANDAR, IR ADIANTE
GO BACK: VOLTAR
GOOD AFTERNOON: BOA TARDE
GOOD COEXISTENCE RULES: REGRAS DE BOA CONVIVÊNCIA
GOOD EVENING: BOA NOITE
GOOD MORNING: BOM DIA
GOOD NIGHT: BOA NOITE (NA DESPEDIDA)
GOODIES: COISAS BOAS, GULOSEIMAS
GRANDMA: AVÓ
GRANDPA: AVÔ
GRAY: CINZA
GREEN: VERDE
GROW: CRESCER

H

HAIR: CABELO

HAND: MÃO
HAPPY: FELIZ
HAPPY BIRTHDAY: FELIZ ANIVERSÁRIO
HAVE: TER
HAVE A BREAK: FAZER UMA PAUSA
HAVE FUN: DIVERTIR-SE
HE: ELE
HEAD: CABEÇA
HEALTHY: SAUDÁVEL
HELLO: OLÁ, OI
HERE: AQUI
HI: OI, OLÁ
HILL: MORRO, MONTANHA
HIS: DELE
HOME: CASA; LAR
HOMEWORK: LIÇÃO DE CASA
HOSPITAL: HOSPITAL
HOT: QUENTE
HOUSE: CASA
HUNGRY: COM FOME; FAMINTO

I

I: EU
I'M: EU SOU; ESTOU
IN: EM; DENTRO DE
IN PAIRS: EM DUPLAS
INTERVIEW: ENTREVISTAR; ENTREVISTA
IS: É; ESTÁ
IT: ELE; ELA (ANIMAIS E OBJETOS)
IT'S: ELE(A) É; ESTÁ

J

JACK STONE: CINCO MARIAS
JUICE: SUCO
JUNGLE: SELVA

Ilustrações: Ciau Souza/Arquivo da editora

ONE HUNDRED AND NINE **109**

K

KEEP: MANTER
KIDS: CRIANÇAS
KITCHEN: COZINHA

KITE: PIPA
KNOW: CONHECER

L

LASER STRING GAME: JOGO DE FIOS DE LASER
LEARN: APRENDER
LEG: PERNA
LET'S: VAMOS
LETTUCE: ALFACE
LIKE: GOSTAR
LIME: LIMÃO
LISTEN: OUVIR
LIVING ROOM: SALA DE VISITAS
LOOK: OLHAR
LOVE: AMAR
LUNCH BOX: LANCHEIRA

M

MAKE: FAZER
MATCH: LIGAR; RELACIONAR
MILK: LEITE
MISS A TURN: PERDER A VEZ
MISSING: FALTANDO
MOBILE GAME: JOGO DE CELULAR
MOM: MAMÃE
MOON: LUA
MOUTH: BOCA
MUSEUM: MUSEU
MY: MEU; MINHA

N

NAME: NOME
NIGHT: NOITE
NINE: NOVE
NINETEEN: DEZENOVE
NO: NÃO
NOSE: NARIZ

NOTEBOOK: CADERNO
NOTES: ANOTAÇÕES
NUMBER: NÚMERO

O

ODD: ESTRANHO
OF: DE
ON: SOBRE; EM CIMA
ONION: CEBOLA
OR: OU
ORANGE: LARANJA (FRUTA; COR)
ORANGE JUICE: SUCO DE LARANJA
OUR: NOSSO(A)
OVAL: OVAL
OVEN: FOGÃO

P

PAPAYA: MAMÃO
PAPER: PAPEL
PARK: PARQUE
PARROT: PAPAGAIO
PEACH: PÊSSEGO
PEAR: PÊRA
PEDESTRIAN: PEDESTRE

PEN: CANETA

PENCIL: LÁPIS
PENCIL CASE: ESTOJO DE LÁPIS

PENCIL SHARPENER: APONTADOR
PET SHOP: LOJA DE ANIMAIS
PICTURE: FIGURA; FOTO
PIGEON: POMBO
PINK: COR-DE-ROSA
PLACE: LUGAR
PLANT: PLANTAR
PLATE: PRATO
PLAY: BRINCAR
PLAY TIME: HORA DE BRINCAR
POTATO: BATATA
PROGRESS: PROGRESSO
PUZZLE: QUEBRA-CABEÇA

R

RABBIT: COELHO
RACKETBALL: FRESCOBOL
RADISH: RABANETE
RASPBERRY: FRAMBOESA
REALLY: REALMENTE
RECIPE: RECEITA
RECTANGLE: RETÂNGULO
RED: VERMELHO
RED HAIR: CABELO RUIVO
RED PEPPER: PIMENTÃO VERMELHO
RESPECT: RESPEITAR; RESPEITO
REVIEW: REVISAR; REVISÃO
RICE: ARROZ
ROLLERBLADES: PATINS
ROSE: ROSA
RULES: REGRAS

S

SANDCASTLE: CASTELO DE AREIA

SAY: DIZER; FALAR
SCALE: ESCAMAS
SCHOOL: ESCOLA
SCHOOLBAG: MOCHILA
SCHOOL BUS: ÔNIBUS ESCOLAR
SCHOOL OBJECTS: OBJETOS ESCOLARES
SCIENCE: CIÊNCIAS
SCOOTER: PATINETE
SEA: MAR
SEA ANIMAL: ANIMAL MARINHO
SEA TURTLE: TARTARUGA MARINHA
SEAHORSE: CAVALO-MARINHO
SEARCH: PESQUISAR; PROCURAR
SEASHELL: CONCHA
SEE: VER
SEED: SEMENTE

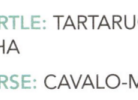

SHARK: TUBARÃO
SHOPPING MALL: CENTRO COMERCIAL; *SHOPPING CENTER*
SHOW: MOSTRAR
SING: CANTAR
SISTER: IRMÃ
SIT: SENTAR
SKATEBOARD: SKATE
SKY: CÉU
SMALL: PEQUENO(A)
SNAIL: CARACOL
SNAKE: COBRA
SNAP: ESTALAR
SO: ASSIM
SOCK PUPPET: FANTOCHE DE MEIA
SOIL: TERRA, SOLO
SOLIDARITY: SOLIDARIEDADE

SOME: ALGUNS
SPORTS CLUB: CLUBE ESPORTIVO
SQUARE: QUADRADO
SQUIRREL: ESQUILO
STAMP: BATER (PÉS)
STAR: ESTRELA

STARFISH: ESTRELA-DO-MAR
START: INICIAR; INÍCIO
STINGRAY: RAIA, ARRAIA
STOP: PARAR; PARE
STRAWBERRY: MORANGO
SUGAR: AÇÚCAR
SUN: SOL
SUNGLASSES: ÓCULOS DE SOL
SUNSCREEN: PROTETOR SOLAR
SUPERMARKET: SUPERMERCADO
SWEET: DOCE

T

TAKE CARE: CUIDAR; CUIDE-SE
TEACHER: PROFESSOR(A)
TEAMWORK: TRABALHO EM EQUIPE
THANKS: OBRIGADO(A)
THE: O(A); OS(AS)
THEM: ELES(AS)
THERE: LÁ
THIRSTY: COM SEDE
THIS: ESTE(A)
TIC-TAC TOE BOARD: TABULEIRO DE JOGO DA VELHA
TIDY UP: LIMPAR, ORGANIZAR
TIN CAN PHONE: TELEFONE SEM FIO
TODAY: HOJE
TOE(S): DEDO(S) DO(S) PÉ(S)

TOILET SEAT: VASO SANITÁRIO
TOY: BRINQUEDO
TRAFFIC LIGHTS: SEMÁFORO
TREE: ÁRVORE
TRIANGLE: TRIÂNGULO
TURTLE: TARTARUGA

U

URBAN: URBANO
USE: USAR

V

VEGETABLE: LEGUMES, VEGETAIS

W

WANT: QUERER
WASTE: DESPERDIÇAR; DESPERDÍCIO; LIXO
WATER: ÁGUA
WATER BOTTLE: GARRAFA DE ÁGUA
WELCOME: BEM-VINDO
WHAT: O QUE, QUAL
WHERE: ONDE
WHITE: BRANCO
WILD ANIMALS: ANIMAIS SILVESTRES
WINDOW SHOP: VITRINE
WITH: COM
WORD: PALAVRA
WORK IN GROUPS: TRABALHAR EM GRUPOS
WRITE: ESCREVER

Y

YARD: QUINTAL
YELLOW: AMARELO
YES: SIM
YOU: VOCÊ
YOUR: SEU; SUA

STRUCTURES

EM INGLÊS DIZEMOS:	PARA DIZER:
WHAT IS IT?	O QUE É ISTO?
IT IS A DOLL.	É UMA BONECA.
WHAT'S YOUR NAME?	QUAL É O SEU NOME?
MY NAME IS KITTY.	MEU NOME É KITTY.
WHAT COLOR IS THE SUN?	DE QUE COR É O SOL?
IT IS YELLOW.	ELE É AMARELO.
WHAT COLOR ARE THE BALLOONS?	QUAL É A COR DOS BALÕES?
THE BALLOONS ARE BLUE.	OS BALÕES SÃO AZUIS.
WHERE IS LEO?	ONDE ESTÁ LEO?
LEO IS IN THE PARK.	LEO ESTÁ NO PARQUE.
WHAT ANIMAL IS IT?	QUE ANIMAL É ESTE?
IS IT A SNAKE?	É UMA COBRA?
YES, IT IS. / NO, IT ISN'T.	SIM, É. / NÃO, NÃO É.
WHAT IS YOUR FAVORITE PLACE?	QUAL É O SEU LUGAR FAVORITO?
LET'S GO TO THE BEACH! / COUNTRYSIDE!	VAMOS PARA A PRAIA! / O CAMPO!
GOOD EVENING. / GOOD NIGHT.	BOA NOITE. / BOA NOITE (NA DESPEDIDA).
ARE YOU HUNGRY, ALLAN?	VOCÊ ESTÁ COM FOME, ALLAN?
ARE YOU THIRSTY, KITTY?	VOCÊ ESTÁ COM SEDE, KITTY?
EAT YOUR BREAKFAST, DEAR.	TOME SEU CAFÉ DA MANHÃ, QUERIDO(A).
MY EYES ARE BLUE.	MEUS OLHOS SÃO AZUIS.
MY HAIR IS BLACK.	MEU CABELO É PRETO.

UNIT 1 MY FAVORITE TOYS

NAME: _____

CLASS: _____ **DATE:** __/__/__

1. MATCH.

 •   KITE   •

         MOBILE GAME

 •   PUZZLE   •

         CHESS   •

 •   COSTUME

         SKATEBOARD   •

         SCOOTER   •

 •

2. WRITE.

WHAT IS YOUR FAVORITE TOY?

MY FAVORITE TOY IS THE _____.

3. COLOR. WHAT COLOR ARE THE SHAPES?

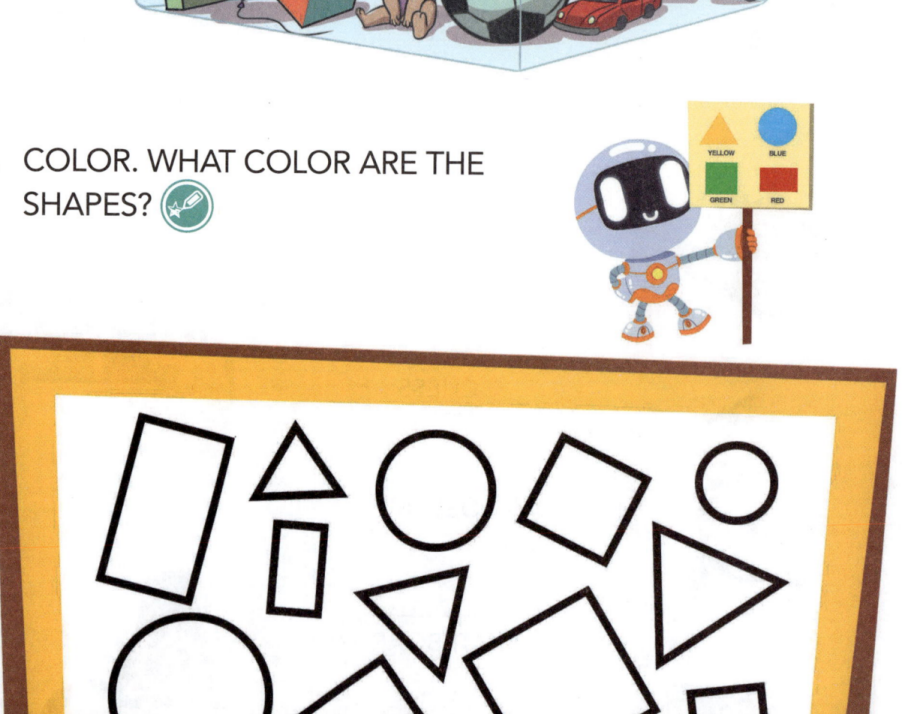

UNIT 2 THE BROWN'S HOME

NAME: _____

CLASS: _____ **DATE:** ___/___/___

1. LOOK AND NUMBER. ✏️

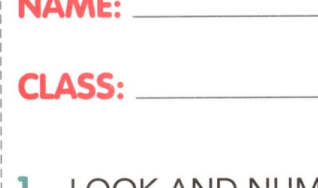

_____

1 BATHROOM

2 LIVING ROOM

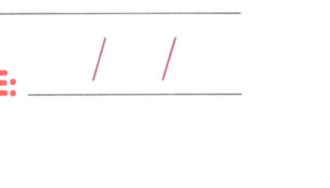

_____

_____

3 KITCHEN

4 GARDEN

_____

_____

5 BEDROOM

6 YARD

_____

2. MATCH AND WRITE.

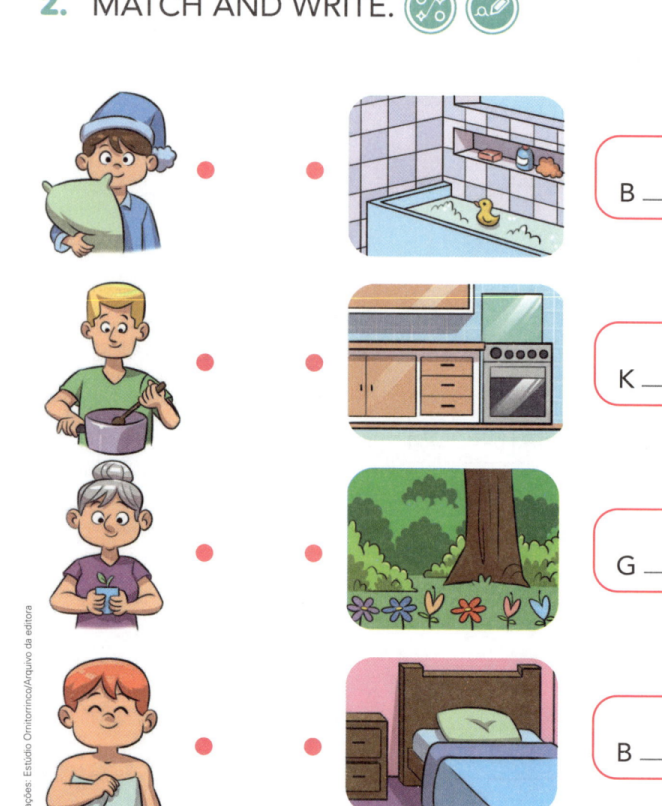

B ____ TH ____ ____ ____ M

K ____ ____ CH ____ N

G ____ ____ D ____ N

B ____ D ____ ____ ____ M

3. COLOR BY NUMBER.

Number	Color
1	**RED**
2	**BLUE**
3	**PINK**
4	**BROWN**
5	**GREEN**
6	**YELLOW**

UNIT 3 GOOD AFTERNOON, TEACHER!

NAME: _____

CLASS: _____ **DATE:** ___/___/___

1. READ AND CIRCLE.

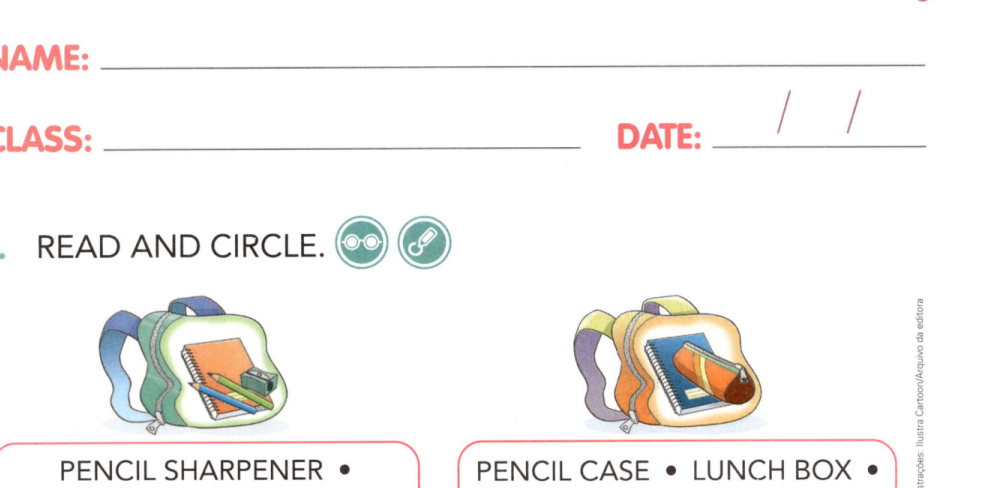

PENCIL SHARPENER • NOTEBOOK • PEN • PENCIL

PENCIL CASE • LUNCH BOX • NOTEBOOK • BOOK

PENCIL • ERASER • NOTEBOOK • PEN

PENCIL • PENCIL CASE • PEN • BOOK

2. MATCH THE NUMBERS.

Number	Word
3 •	• TWELVE
8 •	• SEVEN
12 •	• THREE
10 •	• SIX
7 •	• EIGHT
6 •	• TEN

3. COUNT AND WRITE.

____ ____ ____ ____ ERASERS

____ ____ ____ PENCIL CASES

____ ____ ____ SCHOOLBAGS

____ ____ ____ ____ ____ PENS

____ ____ ____ ____ NOTEBOOKS

____ ____ ____ PENCILS

4. COLOR THE SCHOOL OBJECTS.

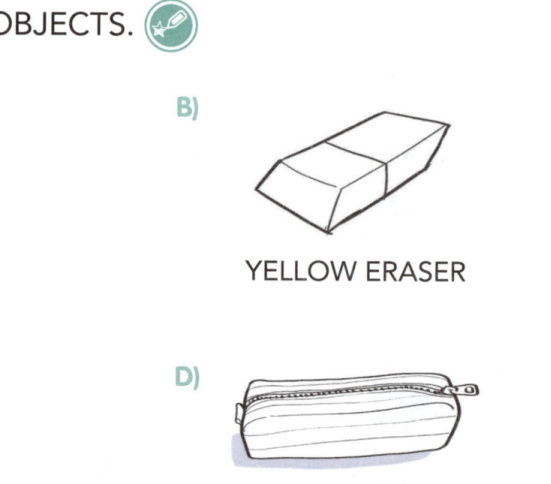

A) RED PEN

B) YELLOW ERASER

C) PINK LUNCH BOX

D) ORANGE PENCIL CASE

WORKBOOK

UNIT 4 AROUND THE CITY

NAME: _____

CLASS: _____ **DATE:** ___/___/___

1. MATCH.

- SCHOOL
- SHOPPING MALL
- PET SHOP
- HOSPITAL
- SUPERMARKET
- MUSEUM

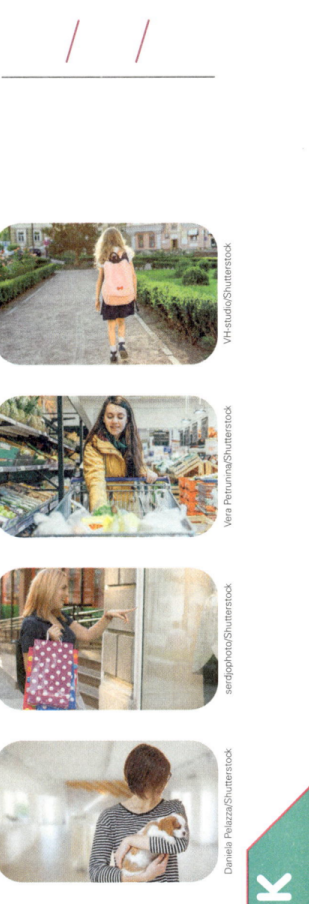

2. MAKE AN X AND CIRCLE.

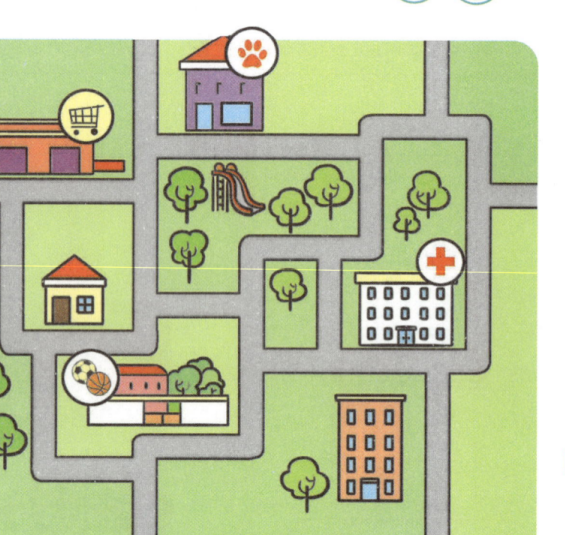

SUPERMARKET	○
MUSEUM	○
HOSPITAL	○
PET SHOP	○
PARK	○
SHOPPING MALL	○
SPORTS CLUB	○

3. READ AND WRITE.

PARK • SHOPPING MALL • MUSEUM

WHERE IS JESSICA?

JESSICA IS IN THE _____.

WHERE IS MARK?

MARK IS IN THE _____.

WHERE IS RACHEL?

RACHEL IS IN THE _____.

WORKBOOK

UNIT 5 AT THE BEACH

NAME: _____

CLASS: _____ **DATE:** ____/____/____

1. NUMBER AND COLOR.

1 CLOUD	3 SUN	5 SEASHELL
2 SEA	4 SANDCASTLE	6 STARFISH

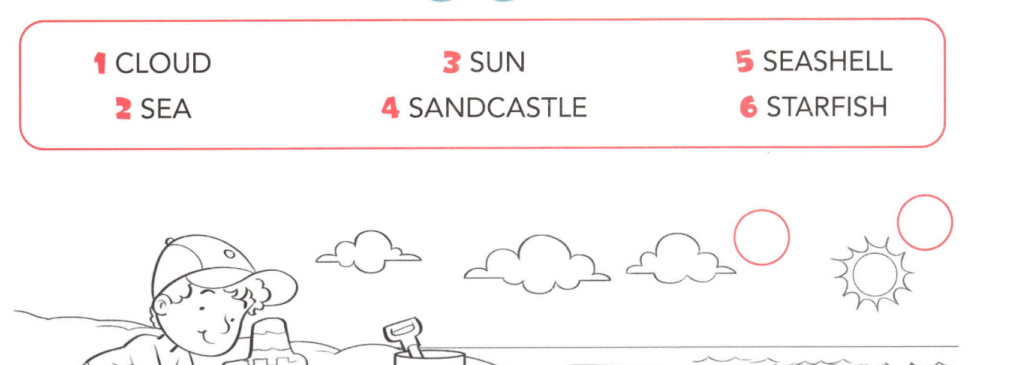

2. CIRCLE AND WRITE.

3. READ AND WRITE. 👀 ✏️

BLUE • GREEN • ORANGE • PINK • RED • YELLOW

A) WHAT COLOR IS THE SUN?

IT'S _____.

B) WHAT COLOR IS THE STARFISH?

IT'S _____.

C) WHAT COLOR IS THE SEASHELL?

IT'S _____.

D) WHAT COLOR IS THE FISH?

IT'S _____.

E) WHAT COLOR IS THE DOLPHIN?

IT'S _____.

F) WHAT COLOR IS THE SKY?

IT'S _____.

WORKBOOK

UNIT 6 I LOVE ANIMALS!

NAME: _____

CLASS: _____ **DATE:** ____ / ____

1. READ AND WRITE.

ANT • BEE • SNAIL • SQUIRREL

A) WHAT IS THIS?

IT'S A _____.

B) WHAT IS THIS?

IT'S AN _____.

C) WHAT IS THIS?

IT'S A _____.

D) WHAT IS THIS?

IT'S A _____.

2. COUNT AND WRITE.

_____ONE_____ RABBIT

_____ PARROTS

_____ SNAKES

_____ FROGS

_____ FISH

3. READ, COLOR AND WRITE.

(BEE • FROG • PARROT • RABBIT • SNAKE)

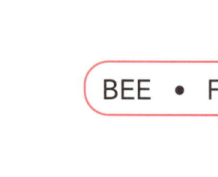

I AM A _____FISH_____.
I AM BLUE.

I AM A _____.
I AM GREEN.

I AM A _____.
I AM YELLOW AND BLACK.

I AM A _____.
I AM ORANGE.

I AM A _____.
I AM RED, YELLOW AND BLUE.

I AM A _____.
I AM BROWN AND WHITE.

UNIT 7 TIME FOR BREAKFAST

NAME: ___

CLASS: ___ **DATE:** ___ / ___

1. NUMBER. 🔟

1 EGG	4 MILK	7 ORANGE JUICE
2 SUGAR	5 BANANA	8 BREAD
3 BUTTER	6 APPLE	9 COFFEE

2. WRITE.

APPLES • BANANAS • BREAD • BUTTER • CAKE • COFFEE • EGGS • MILK • ORANGES • SUGAR

3. COUNT AND WRITE.

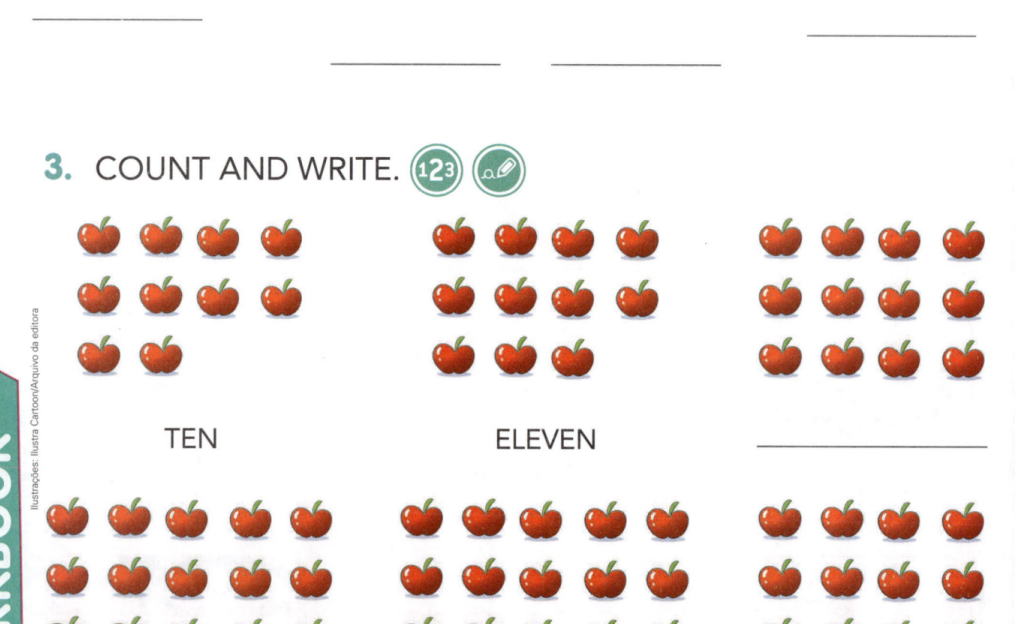

TEN   ELEVEN

EIGHTEEN   SIXTEEN

WORKBOOK

OUR BODY

NAME: _____

CLASS: _____ **DATE:** _____/ /

1. WORDSEARCH. FIND AND CIRCLE.

ARMS • EARS • EYES • FINGERS • FOOT • HANDS • HEAD • LEG • MOUTH • NOSE • TOES

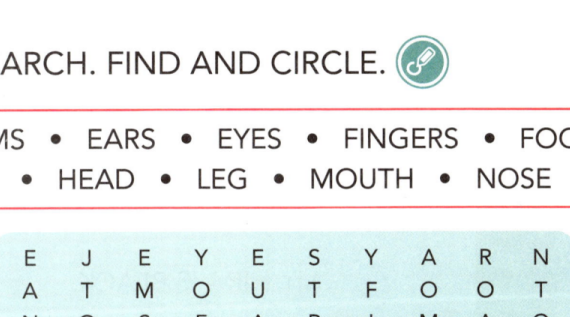

E	J	E	Y	E	S	Y	A	R	N
A	T	M	O	U	T	F	O	O	T
N	O	S	E	A	R	I	M	A	O
O	E	M	J	H	A	N	D	S	Y
H	S	T	S	E	A	G	O	I	A
E	M	E	T	T	L	E	G	U	R
A	R	E	A	R	S	R	M	I	M
D	J	K	V	Y	N	S	J	O	S
F	M	O	U	T	H	A	S	E	A

2. WRITE ABOUT YOU. THEN DRAW YOURSELF.

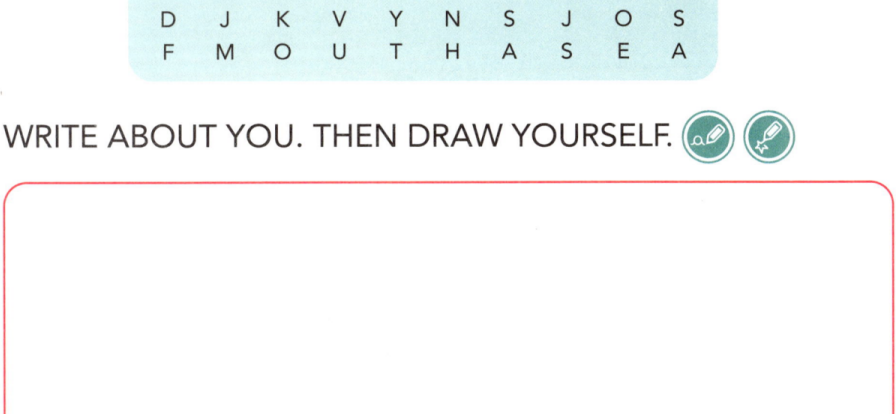

HELLO! MY NAME IS _____.

MY EYES ARE _____. MY HAIR IS _____.

3. UNSCRAMBLE, WRITE AND MATCH.

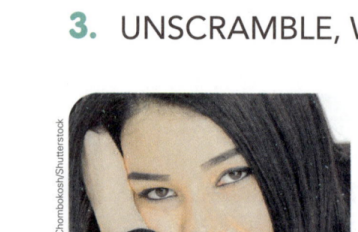

MY **SYEE** ARE GREEN.

MY ____ ____ ____ ____ ARE GREEN.

MY **HIRA** IS BLACK.

MY ____ ____ ____ ____ IS BLACK.

4. COUNT AND NUMBER.

HELLO! I'M KORKY, THE MONSTER!

I HAVE...

NOSES	⃝	HANDS	⃝
HEAD	⃝	LEG	⃝
EYES	⃝	FOOT	⃝
EARS	⃝	TOES	⃝
ARMS	⃝	FINGERS	⃝
		MOUTHS	⃝

WORKBOOK

CELEBRATION CRAFTS

HAPPY EASTER!

HAPPY FRIENDSHIP DAY!

HAPPY MOTHER'S DAY!

HAPPY FATHER'S DAY!

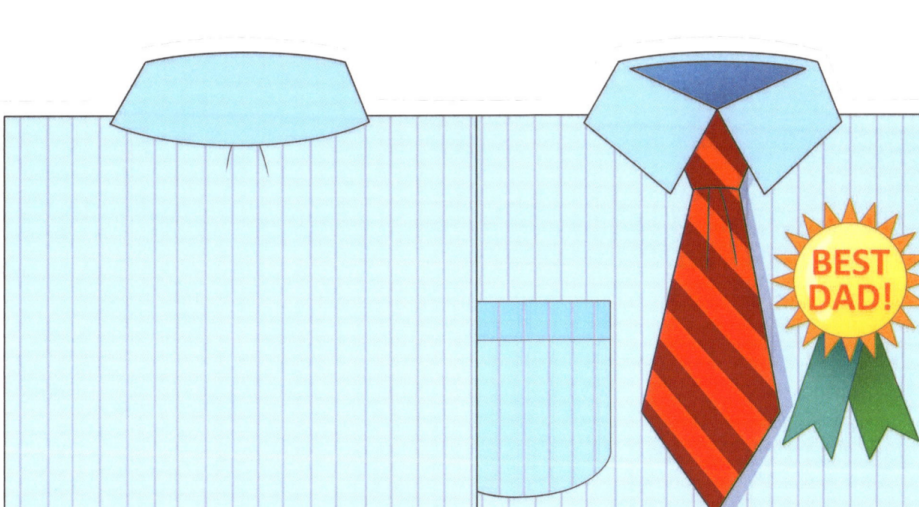

HAPPY THANKSGIVING DAY!

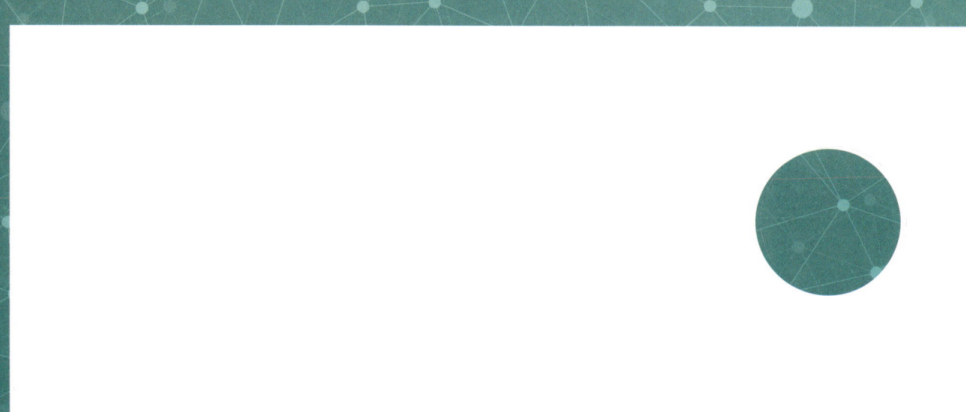

MERRY CHRISTMAS AND HAPPY NEW YEAR!

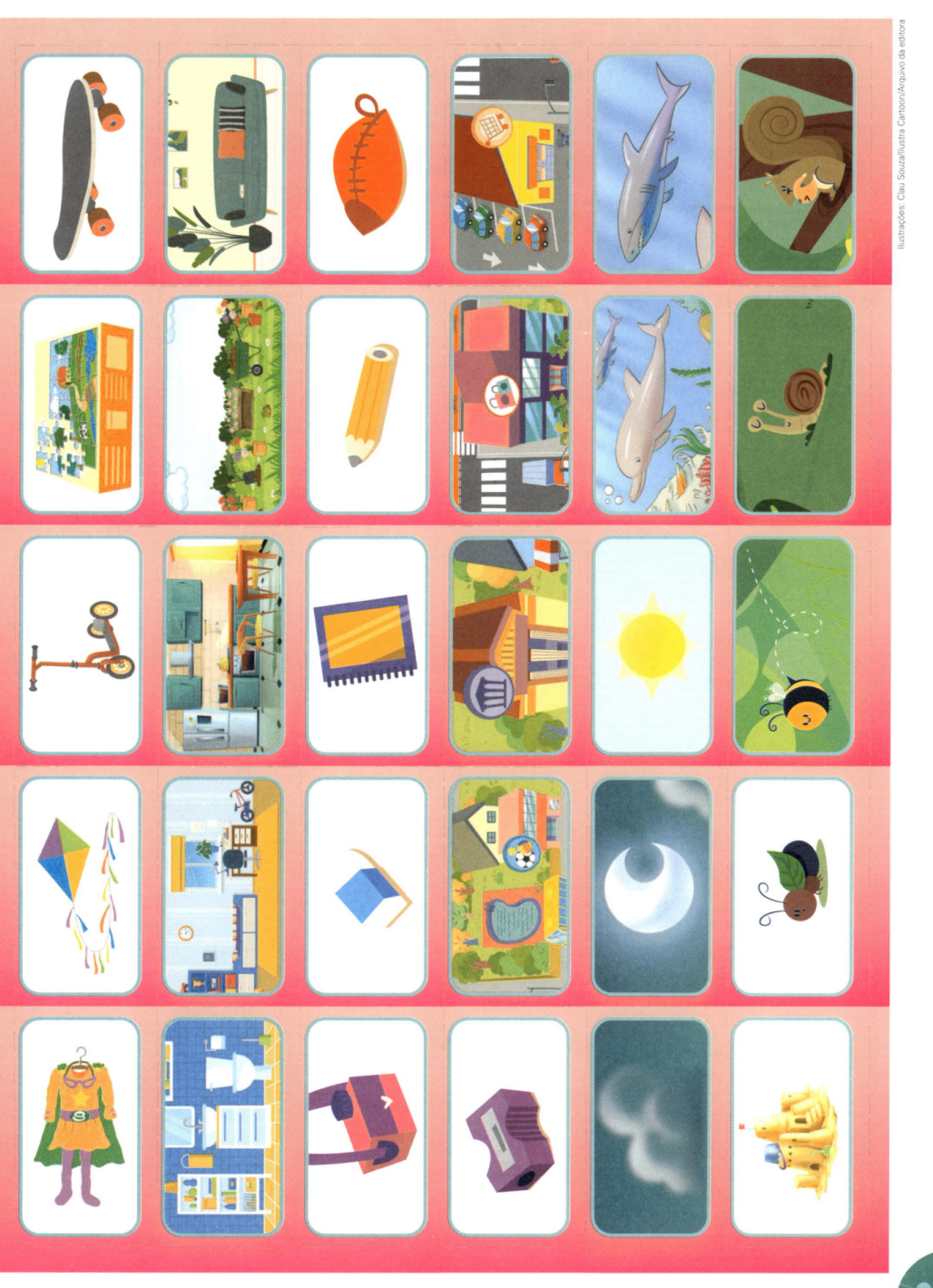

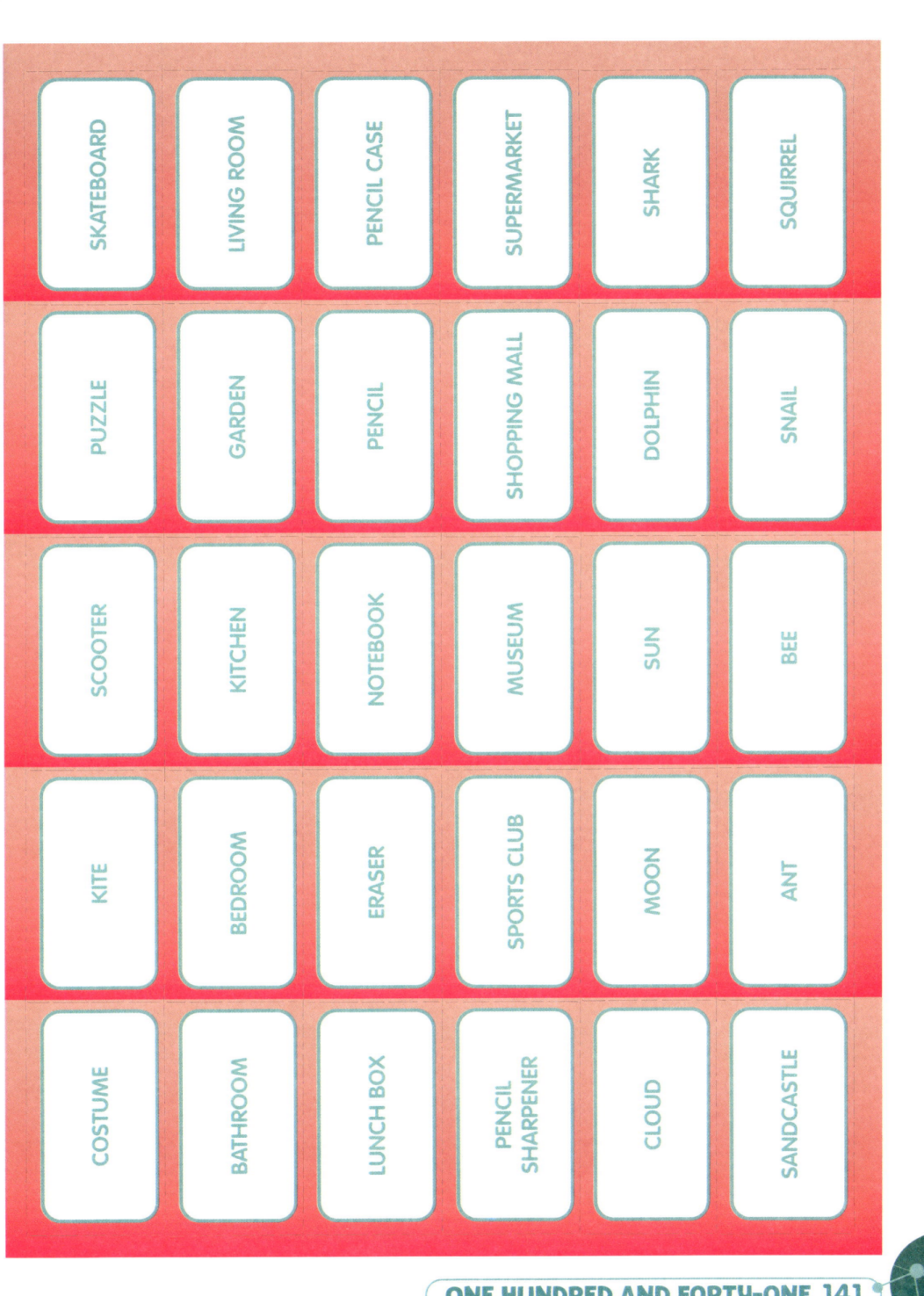

			BUTTER	EYE	HEAD
			BREAD	EAR	FINGER
		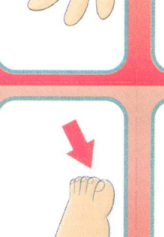	PARROT	SUGAR	TOE
			SNAKE	MILK	NOSE
			FROG	COFFEE	MOUTH

STICKERS

NAME: _____	NAME: _____
CLASS: _____	CLASS: _____

NAME: _____	NAME: _____
CLASS: _____	CLASS: _____

PAGES 8 AND 9

PAGE 10

PAGES 18 AND 19

PAGE 20

PAGES 30 AND 31

PAGE 32

PAGES 40 AND 41

PAGE 42

PAGES 52 AND 53

PAGES 54 AND 55

PAGES 62 AND 63

PAGES 74 AND 75

PAGE 64

PAGE 76

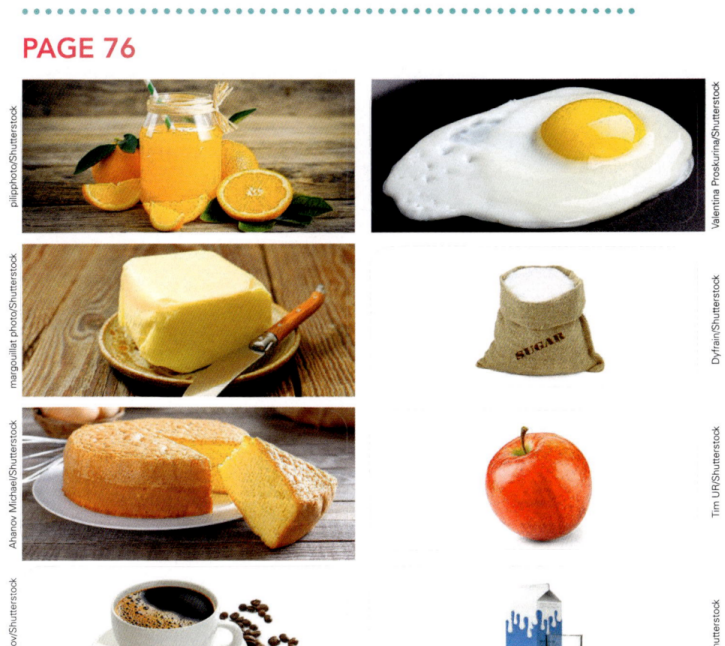

PAGES 84 AND 85

PAGE 86

HAIR	HEAD	MOUTH
HAND	FINGER	EYE
LEG	FOOT	TOE
ARM	NOSE	EAR